TH
FOOTBALL DIET
AND FITNESS PROGRAMME

Jane Nottage was liaison manager for Italia '90, the World Cup Organising Committee, and was assigned to the England team for the duration of the World Cup finals that year. She was personal assistant and commercial manager to Paul Gascoigne when he joined Lazio in 1992. She is the author of *The Italians* and *Paul Gascoigne, The Inside Story*.

Dr Claudio Bartolini is in charge of Lazio's medical department. An active sportsman in his youth, he developed a special interest in sports injuries during his medical training. In 1975 he joined Lazio as the youth-team doctor, then spent six years with the Football Federation as the medical adviser in charge of the amateur league before rejoining Lazio in 1989.

Beppe Signori is Lazio's star striker, and was the leading 'Serie A' goalscorer during the 1992–93 season. He was bought by Lazio in 1992, leaving his first club, Foggia, and immediately triumphed in terms of scoring goals and performance.

THE ITALIAN
FOOTBALL DIET
AND FITNESS PROGRAMME

Jane Nottage and Dr Claudio Bartolini

Thorsons
An Imprint of HarperCollinsPublishers

Thorsons
An imprint of HarperCollins*Publishers*
77–85 Fulham Palace Road,
Hammersmith, London W6 8JB
1160 Battery Street,
San Francisco, California 94111–1213

Published by Thorsons 1994

1 3 5 7 9 10 8 6 4 2

A catalogue record for this book
is available from the British Library

ISBN 0 7225 2950 3

Printed in Great Britain by
HarperCollinsManufacturing Glasgow

CONTENTS

ACKNOWLEDGEMENTS

The authors would like to thank the following people: Gloria Ferdinandi, a dietitian based in Rome and colleague of Dr Bartolini, who specialises in diets for athletes; Fiona Hayes, freelance fitness consultant, who trains and examines YMCA exercise instructors, and is an experienced fitness instructor in many sports; Gino Santin, restauranteur and expert on Italian football.

The publishers would like to thank the following people: Jill Horgan, Jane Griffin, Liz Godfray and Bridget Jones.

Jane Nottage would like to dedicate this book to Terry Venables, whose courage and tenacity should be an inspiration to us all.

FOREWORD

by Beppe Signori

Over the last ten years, fitness has become a significant consideration for more and more people, not just top athletes. And to complement the fitness regime, diet is an integral part of any sporting lifestyle.

In Italy, mealtimes are a valued ritual, an opportunity to gather around the table with family and friends and enjoy good, wholesome food. For many years Italy was known for its food rather than its healthy lifestyle, but now it has been acknowledged that our diet is not only mouth-watering, but is also essentially healthy and the best choice for athletes.

We Italian footballers are educated from an early age to take our diet seriously. Most teams employ a dietitian, whose job it is to monitor our dietary needs on an individual basis, taking into consideration any adaptation that may be required as the season progresses.

Dedication and discipline are important parts of our lives. We all like good food, but we realise the importance of eating the right foods in the right amounts. I am an athlete and I never forget it. My body and the state it is in is vital to my job. If I do not train for a day or two, I can put on enough weight for it to have a disastrous effect on my overall performance on the pitch. So I watch what I eat and I eat regularly. Lunch is at 12.30–1 p.m., and dinner always around 8–8.30 p.m. My friends have got used to this – they accept that it is a part of my lifestyle that I will not change. This does not mean that I cannot have the occasional 'blow out'. We are allowed a certain number of 'free' meals during the season, when we can eat whatever we like. I save these up for when I visit my mother, and can enjoy a bit of home cooking. I come from Bergamo in northern Italy, where fairly heavy foods like polenta – my favourite – are popular, so I have to be careful not to overdo it!

As I also play for the Italian national team, I have to put extra emphasis on fitness and diet. There is no time in my schedule for being tired or lethargic. When we travel, we take our own pasta, olive oil, mineral water and chef to ensure that our dietary regime is not upset. I am not suggesting that you do this every time you go abroad, but whether you are training for something specific, or just a very active sportsperson, be careful not to overturn your basic diet completely every time you travel.

A balanced diet is part of my life – it should be part of yours too. Eating well means living well, and for me that also means playing well. Just turn over the pages and get started on an exciting new approach to optimum health and fitness.

INTRODUCTION

Italy has won the World Cup three times, in 1934, 1938 and 1982. Fitness and diet are important elements in this short, intense competition where teams may be playing several times a week. As Watford manager Glenn Roeder said when he visited Rome in 1991, 'If the English lived like the Italians we would have won the World Cup three or four times.' The dedication and professionalism of the Italians – who always put on their best performance – has made them one of the most successful sporting nations in the world.

Italian football has now captured the imagination of more people than ever before. A 'Serie A' (first division) match is broadcast live on British television every week. We have been enthralled by the technical skill and high quality of these games as well as the stamina and pace demonstrated by the players.

A Winning Formula

Footballers in Italy reach their high level of general fitness through hard work and discipline as well as a great deal of determination. A healthy mental attitude is valued as highly in Italy as an excellent physique, and achieving it is one of the prime objectives of the diet and training regime. Even before it became fashionable to talk about an holistic approach to life, the Italian sportspeople were living the ideal.

This attitude is carried over to every part of the lifestyle, from training to life away from the pitch. The overall philosophy is that balance is the key to fitness – enjoy your life but do everything in moderation. Never is this approach more apparent than in the diet. A balanced diet will help sportspeople attain their highest physical level.

How the Italian Approach Can Help You

This book is not just for footballers. It will help *all* active people attain their peak performance level. Whether you are a professional athlete or someone who just heads for the squash courts twice a week, you will benefit greatly by following the diet and training programme used by professional footballers in Italy.

Several British footballers who have played in Italy

have benefited from the regime. Liam Brady and Ray Wilkins have both declared publicly how the diet helped them achieve a higher level of general fitness. By following the general guidelines in this book, you will soon experience a fitter, healthier lifestyle.

Diet is important for three main reasons:

1 It gives athletes the right mental attitude – respect for their body.
2 A correct diet allows the athlete to train and recover from training, and it is only through a well-devised training programme that performance can improve.
3 Feeding the body with the right nutrients allows the athletes to approach the match in peak physical condition.

A sportsperson's active life can be cut short through illness and injury. By following the basic principles in this book you can help provide your body with the right nutrients to help it fight colds and flu, and keep it in optimum condition. Your body is a machine, and it is important to learn how to look after it. If you treat it well, it will reward you. If you neglect it by eating the wrong food at irregular hours, you will not get the best out of it. To succeed at any sport, it is not enough to be gifted – you must also be self-disciplined and single-minded.

Diet and training are of paramount importance for all Italian football teams, but this does not mean that following their regime cannot be fun. This book challenges the belief that diets are boring and that they make you feel hungry all the time. Athletes cannot afford to have hunger pangs, as much as they cannot afford to carry excess weight. By eating the right foods regularly and 'refuelling' the body sensibly, they can delay the effects of ageing and prolong their careers. Some players have ignored their bodies and continued to live erratically. These are the bright stars who shine briefly before fading into obscurity. Now, by reading this book, you can share the secrets of the real stars, the most successful and enduring players.

The book will deal with basic nutritional requirements and take you through the dietary guidelines followed by the Italian teams. You can discover the 'superfood' for sportspeople and learn what the stars eat and how they train. This is the only in-depth diet for active sportspeople. It will help you to plan your activity and to eat what you need to succeed at it. You do not have to be a professional athlete to benefit from the Serie A diet and fitness programme. It is your way to maximise your sporting potential.

Ten Golden Rules for a Fitter Life

1. Lead a regular lifestyle. Anyone who wishes to live well should attempt to lead a balanced life. Worry and anxiety put the body under stress, as do smoking and too much alcohol. Erratic eating habits – skipping meals, eating a lot at one meal and nothing at the next – do nothing to help the body adjust to the demands of an active existence. Only by following the essential rules of balance and harmony will we really get the best out of our bodies. An holistic approach to life means that your mind, body and spirit are in harmony. If there is a great difference between one or the other, then the neglected part will always try and compensate, causing anxiety or illness.

2. Take regular exercise and follow a good diet. This will lead to better overall health and happiness.

3. Chew your food slowly (at least 50 times). This helps to stimulate digestion.

4. Make sure that you drink plenty of fluids. If you sweat significantly during exercise, drink up to 1¼ pints (1 litre) in the 2–3 hours before activity.

5. Spread your daily intake of food over three full meals and two snacks.

6. Be aware of the fats you eat (see page 14).

7. Do not weigh yourself every day. Weight always varies from day to day. There is no point in starving yourself because you have gained a little weight from one day to the next. In some cases,

this can lead to a negative bingeing–starving syndrome. This advice is particularly important for women who tend to put on weight just before menstruation due to water-retention.

8 Vary your diet. Your food and the way it is cooked must never be monotonous. The brain has an important function in stimulating appetite. To gain maximum benefit from food, we should find it attractive.

9 Give precedence in your diet to foods that feature in the Mediterranean-style diet – pasta, wholemeal bread, fish, beans, fruit and vegetables.

10 Take a multivitamin tablet daily, especially when in the training phase of activity.

WARNING

Before starting any strenuous training programme or dietary regime, it is important to
discuss your plans with your doctor. This is vital
if any of the following apply to you:

- High blood pressure or any cardio-vascular
  problem.
- A family history of heart disease.
- Unaccountable chest pains or tightness,
  especially if this happens after little effort.
- A tendency to headaches, fainting or dizziness.
- Any medical problem that may interfere with
  participation in an exercise programme.
- Pain or limited movement in any joint.
- You are currently taking drugs or medication.
- You are extremely overweight or under-
  weight.
- You are new to exercise and over 40 years of
  age.
- You are pregnant.

1

THE SPORTS SUPERDIET

The Mediterranean-style diet is balanced and healthy. It is the best option for everyone – and has many advantages for the active sportsperson. The main elements are pasta, bread, milk products such as yoghurt and cheese, fish, fruit, vegetables, and a reasonable, but not excessive, amount of meat. It is the ideal way to provide the body with the right proportions of the main nutrients.

Unlike some foods, simple Italian 'country' cooking does not involve rich, creamy sauces and calorie-laden sweets. It is only with the influence of the wealthy that the Italian diet has suffered, bringing with it the so-called 'diseases of the rich'. Studies conducted by well-known American nutritionist Ancel Keys have revealed that a diet typical of that found in the Mediterranean area coincides with a reduction in certain diseases, such as high blood pressure, heart attacks, obesity, digestive problems and diabetes, which are all common in the USA and other highly industrialised nations.

As well as providing all the essential nutrients, the

Mediterranean-style diet is also very appealing. It can hardly be described as a hardship to have to eat plates of pasta with fresh tomato sauce and basil, or freshly grilled fish with herbs, a large dish of salad and some bread.

What Does Your Body Need?

There are two considerations when preparing a balanced diet for the athlete: how to provide enough food to give a greater energy value than that needed by a less active person; and how to provide the necessary amount of high-quality food. The dietary guidelines throughout this book, and the recipes in Chapter Five, have been carefully prepared with these considerations in mind.

Energy

Athletes use up more energy than most people. An activity that involves three or four hours of intense training every day can require a daily intake of 3,500–4,000 calories. The amount of energy expended varies between men and women and between sports (see Figure 1.1).

Team sports generally use up fewer calories, as not all the team is involved in constant action; there are rest periods when the players can pace themselves. The amount of energy used in playing football is about

SPORT	MEN	WOMEN
Archery	420	268
Basketball (moderate)	575	352
Canoeing (4 mph/6.5 km/h)	565	352
Cycling (5.5 mph/9 km/h on level ground)	409	251
Dancing (moderate)	341	209
Fencing (moderate)	409	251
Football	730	447
Golf (twosome)	443	271
Handball (vigorous)	797	488
Mountain climbing	820	503
Riding (trot)	551	338
Rowing (20 strokes/minute)	1116	684
Running (5.5 mph/9 km/h)	887	537
Skiing (downhill)	789	483
Squash	849	520
Swimming (competitive; crawl)	869	532
Tennis (moderate)	565	347
Volleyball (moderate)	465	285
Walking (4.5 mph/7 km/h)	540	331
Water skiing	638	391
Wrestling, judo or karate	1049	643

Figure 1.1. Approximate number of calories used per hour in different sports for men and women. The calories given for men are based on those required by a 205-lb (93-kg) male; those for women, on an 125-lb (57-kg) female. (This information taken from Grandjean A.C.: Nutrition for Sport Success. Reston, VA, The American Alliance for Health, Physical Education, Recreation and Dance, 1984, p.6.)

average; a footballer's diet therefore provides a good basis that can be adapted by other athletes to suit their needs.

Energy requirements also depend on the phase of the training. The most intense is the preparation period, during which the body has to work hardest, especially after a period of rest. For footballers, the training period after the summer holidays is a crucial time.

A Balanced Diet

Sportspeople often mistakenly believe that, because they expend a lot of energy, they can get away with filling themselves up with chocolates and fatty foods. The Italian footballers' diet does not work on these principles. It stresses the importance of keeping to a *healthy* diet and augmenting the intake of foods where necessary, but only foods that are part of a normal, balanced diet.

The Essential Nutrients

Carbohydrates

Carbohydrates are a vital source of energy. The athlete's best friend, they supply the muscles with glycogen – the fuel needed for exercise.

During sporting activity, carbohydrates provide an easily accessible store of energy. The speed at which these stores are used up depends on several factors, including the intensity and duration of exercise. As intensity increases, more carbohydrate is needed to provide a quick release of energy. As intensity drops, fats are pulled in to provide an additional source of fuel. Fats should *not*, however, be increased in the diet, as evidence suggests that they do not provide an adequate substitute for carbohydrates, and increasing their intake can cause health problems (see page 14).

Atheletes need more energy than less active people, and the best way to achieve it is through a diet high in carbohydrates. There are different types of carbohydrates present in food, which can be loosely divided into two groups – starches and sugars. Starch is found (together with fibre) in plants, and is commonly referred to as complex carbohydrate or unrefined, natural carbohydrate. Good sources include:

- pasta
- rice
- bread
- potatoes
- beans
- peas
- lentils
- bananas
- breakfast cereals

Sugars, which taste sweet to varying degrees, are converted to glucose in the body. They are sometimes called simple or refined carbohydrates, and are considered less nutritious from a health point of view than complex carbohydrates. Sources include sugar, sweets, honey and jam.

The athlete's diet should consist of 60–70 per cent carbohydrates. If this high intake were to be achieved through an intake of starchy foods alone, the diet would be extremely bulky in terms of the sheer volume of food that would need to be eaten. This is where the sugary foods are useful, providing a 'top-up' to the carbohydrate levels. Remember, however, that many sweet foods contain fat, so choose carefully and monitor your fat intake (see page 14).

Protein

Protein is essential for life. It is responsible for the growth, repair and maintenance of cells that carry out vital functions, and for the production of enzymes, hormones and other substances that control our hereditary characteristics. Protein is the principal component of muscle tissue, internal organs, skin, hair and parts of the bone.

Approximately 10 per cent of the diet should consist of protein. The best sources are meat, fish, eggs and milk products. This does not mean, however, that sportspeople should fill themselves up with meat and animal fats as these are high in saturated fats and can lead to high cholesterol levels in the blood (see page 26). Good sources of vegetable protein include beans, peas, lentils, nuts, seeds, bread, potatoes, rice, pasta, cereals, soya beans, soya milk and textured vegetable protein.

Fats

Fats are essential for many bodily functions, such as growth, regulation of the cholesterol mechanism, and for maintaining the cell membranes and the elasticity of the skin. Deposits of fat are found under the skin, which help the body maintain a constant internal temperature, and also around vital organs such as the heart and kidneys to help protect them. Fats also have an essential function in transporting the fat-soluble vitamins, such as A, D, E and K, around the body.

Approximately 25–30 per cent of the total energy content of the diet should consist of fats. This amount should be the same for everyone – athletes *and* less active people. Fats are a concentrated form of energy, providing more than twice the number of calories as carbohydrates or protein on a weight-for-weight basis. Athletes will not, however, benefit by increasing their consumption of fats at the expense of carbohydrates.

Fat is a fuel, but the body uses it in a very different way to carbohydrates. Even the leanest of athletes will have sufficient stores of fat, and no risk of running out. When it comes to athletic performance, the body's stores of glycogen (supplied by carbohydrates) are much more important. Fat releases energy very slowly, whereas glycogens provide a fast 'top-up'. In a way, carbohydrates give us our speed, but fat allows us to run for longer. Thus sprinters use glycogen exclusively (the race would be over before energy release from fat had hardly got under way) whereas marathon runners use a combination of both, with different proportions of each being used during the race.

As glycogens are so crucial to performance, anything you can do to extend the period before stores become exhausted and fatigue sets in is a priority. Endurance training helps to improve the ability of muscle to use fat, but this relationship is not enhanced, as far as we know, by eating more fat. A low-fat/high-carbohydrate diet is best for performance and is also very much in line with current recommendations for diet in relation to preventing heart disease, cancer and other diseases.

Fats can be obtained from visible and invisible sources. Visible sources, which are easy to see and therefore to avoid, include:

- butter
- margarine
- oils
- lard
- suet
- dripping
- cream
- fatty meat
- poultry skin

As the fat cannot be seen in invisible sources, it is more difficult to avoid. Sources include:

- fat in meat (beef, pork, lamb, bacon, ham)
- cheese
- whole or full-fat milk
- creamy desserts and cheesecake
- meat products (pies, sausages, burgers, pâté, salami)
- chips, crisps, fried food
- nuts, olives, avocado pears
- cakes, biscuits, most types of chocolate
- mayonnaise, creamy sauces

In general, fats that contain a higher percentage of saturated fatty acids are solid at room temperature and found in animal foods such as meat, lard and butter. Fats principally made up of unsaturated fatty acids, such as olive and vegetable oils, are liquid at room temperature. The fats found in chicken and fish, which contain a high proportion of polyunsaturated fatty acids, are exceptions. Olive oil, which is a central part of the Mediterranean-style diet, contains monounsaturated fats. Like polyunsaturated fats, these are preferable to the saturated variety as they are associated with lower levels of blood cholesterol (see page 26).

Vitamins

The discovery and study of vitamins is comparatively recent, and we are still learning about them. Vitamins are essential to many activities in the body, but are necessary in only very small quantities.

Vitamins may be divided into two main groups – fat-soluble and water-soluble. Fat-soluble vitamins can be stored in the body, and it is not always absolutely necessary to include them in the diet every day, whereas water-soluble vitamins need to be topped up daily. Fat-soluble vitamins can build up to toxic levels in the body, so excess doses must not be taken. Vitamin tablets can be damaged by heat or light, so keep them in a sealed container in a cool, dark place. The function of the individual vitamins is shown in Figure 1.2 (see pages 18–20).

Minerals

Minerals also perform vital functions. Animal-based foods such as meat, dairy products and eggs are the best sources of minerals as they generally contain the amounts we need. Unlike vitamins, minerals are not damaged by heat or light, but some may be lost in cooking liquid. The only mineral that is often deficient is iron, particularly in women who menstruate heavily, but supplements should be taken only on doctor's advice. Female and adolescent athletes should also ensure that they have a good dietary intake of calcium, which is needed for healthy bone formation The functions of individual minerals are shown in Figure 1.3 (see pages 21–23).

VITAMIN	FUNCTIONS	SYMPTOMS OF DEFICIT	SOURCES
A	Healthy eyesight, bones and skin.	Poor sight; scaly skin and scalp; spinal infections.	Halibut liver oil, liver, margarine, butter, cheese, eggs.
B_1	Converts glucose into energy in muscles and nerves.	Mental confusion; muscle weakness; cramp; beriberi (rare in Europe and the West).	Dried brewers yeast, yeast extract, brown rice, wheatgerm, nuts, pork.
B_2	Converts protein, fats and sugars into energy; repairs and maintains body tissues and mucous membranes.	Bloodshot eyes; sensitivity to light; scaling of skin on face; hair loss; dizziness; insomnia.	Yeast extract, dried brewers yeast, liver, wheatgerm, cheese, eggs.
B_6	Metabolism of amino acids; formation of brain substances, nerve-impulse transmitters and blood.	Splitting of lips; scaly skin on face; migraine; irritability.	Dried brewers yeast, wheat bran, yeast extract, wheatgerm, oat flakes, pigs liver.

VITAMIN	FUNCTIONS	SYMPTOMS OF DEFICIT	SOURCES
B_{12}	Synthesis of genetic material; efficient action of nervous system.	Tremors; mental disorders; sore tongue; anaemia.	Pigs liver and kidney, fatty fish, pork, beef, lamb, white fish.
C	Maintains collagen, bones and teeth; promotes iron absorption from food; controls blood cholesterol levels; provides resistance to infection.	Weakness; muscle and joint pains; bleeding gums; haemorrhaging; loosening of teeth.	Fresh fruit, especially citrus fruits and green-leafed vegetables.
D	Essential for normal growth of bones.	Growth problems in children; fragility of bones in adults.	Cod liver oil, kippers, mackerel, canned salmon, sardines, tuna, eggs, sunlight (to promote synthesis).

VITAMIN	FUNCTIONS	SYMPTOMS OF DEFICIT	SOURCES
E	Antioxidant; reduces oxygen needs of muscles; maintains healthy blood vessels.	Lethargy; muscle weakness.	Cod liver oil, roasted peanuts, crisps, shrimps, olive oil, green leafy vegetables, fruits, root vegetables.
K	Essential for blood coagulation.	Haemorrhages, especially in new-born babies.	Cauliflower, Brussels sprouts, broccoli, lettuce, spinach, pigs liver, meat, potatoes, pulses (beans).
Niacin	Produces energy from sugars, fats and protein; maintains healthy skin, nerves, brain, tongue and digestive system.	Skin sores; diarrhoea; mental confusion.	Yeast extract, dried brewer's yeast, wheat bran, nuts, pigs liver, chicken, cheese, wholemeal bread.

Figure 1.2. *Actions and sources of major vitamins*

MINERAL	ACTION	SYMPTOMS OF DEFICIT	SOURCES
Calcium	Formation of bones and teeth; coagulation of blood; transmission of nerve impulses.	Rickets in children; bone pain; muscle weakness; spasms.	Cheese, canned fish, nuts, pulses (beans) cows milk, root vegetables.
Phosphorus	Formation of bones and teeth; production of energy	Weakness; bone pain; joint stiffness.	All high-protein foods.
Magnesium	Production of energy; cell replication; growth; transmission of nerve impulses.	Weakness; vertigo; convulsions; cramps; irregular heartbeat; low blood sugar.	Soya beans, nuts, dried brewers yeast, wholewheat flour, brown rice, dried peas, shrimps, green leafy vegetables.
Sodium	Water balance; nervous system functions.	Muscular cramps; mental apathy; reduced appetite.	Yeast extract, bacon, smoked fish, salami, cornflakes, canned or boiled ham, savoury biscuits.

MINERAL	ACTION	SYMPTOMS OF DEFICIT	SOURCES
Potassium	Water balance; enzyme activation.	Vomiting; abdominal distension; paralysis.	Dried fruits, soya flour, molasses, wheat bran, raw salad vegetables, nuts, breakfast cereals.
Chloride	Formation of gastric juices.	Not established.	As for sodium.
Sulphur	Component of active part of muscle fibre.	Relative to the loss of amino acid sulphates.	Mustard powder, dried egg, scallops, lobster, shellfish, crab, garlic, cheese.
Iron	Component of haemoglobin, and other factors involved in metabolism of energy.	Anaemia due to iron deficiency.	Liver, red meat, pulses, cereals, eggs, shellfish, dark-green leafy vegetables.
Zinc	Growth; insulin activity; healthy liver function.	Prevention of growth.	Milk, liver, shellfish.
Iodine	Component of the thyroid hormone.	Thyroid gland problems.	Fish, shellfish, dried brewers yeast, milk, vegetables.

MINERAL	ACTION	SYMPTOMS OF DEFICIT	SOURCES
Copper	Component of enzymes involved in digestion and in the formation of elastin.	Anaemia.	Liver, shellfish, dried brewers yeast, olives, cereals, cherries, pulses, poultry, nuts.
Fluoride	Maintenance of bone and teeth structure.	A higher incidence of tooth decay.	Tea, coffee, shellfish, rice, spinach, onions, lettuce.
Manganese	Component of enzymes of fat synthesis.	Not established.	Cereals, pulses, berries, fruit, tea.
Chromium	Involved in the metabolism of energy and glucose.	Reduction of capacity to metabolise glucose.	Egg yolk, molasses, hard cheese, liver, vegetables, beef, molluscs.
Selenium	Co-enzyme of various vital functions.	Not established.	Fish, poultry, meat, milk, cereals.
Molybdenum	Component of some enzymes from the bodys organs.	Not established.	Pulses, cereals, organ meats, dark-green leafy vegetables.

Figure 1.3. Functions and sources of minerals.

The Sports Superfoods

Pasta

Many people think that pasta was invented by the Italians, but it was actually created by the Chinese. The Italians have developed the various different types of pasta, and have made it famous throughout the world.

Within a balanced diet, pasta is considered the ideal food for sportspeople. There are a number of reasons for this:

1 It is satisfying.
2 It is easily digested and therefore easily absorbed.
3 It is a complex carbohydrate so gives the body a regular amount of energy.
4 It is an excellent food for refuelling the muscles' glycogen stores after exercise.
5 It can form the basis for a complete meal.

Pasta is high in carbohydrate but low in fat, and is also a source of protein (see Figure 1.4). As well as being easy to prepare, which is an important consideration for people with busy lifestyles, pasta is very easy to digest. When dried pasta is cooked, the hard, easily breakable substance becomes gelatinous and soft, making it easily digestible and also very sustaining. As fresh pasta is already quite soft, it needs far less cooking time. Filled pasta, such as ravioli with ricotta cheese and spinach, takes longer to cook than normal pasta. As pasta is so important, there is a whole section

Protein	⅓ oz (8 g)
Fat	⅟₉₀ oz (1 g)
Carbohydrate	1¾ oz (50 g)
Calories	240

Figure 1.4. Nutritional content of 2½ oz (70 g) of dried pasta

in this book on appetising and nutritionally balanced pasta recipes (see Chapter Five).

Italian footballers invariably have a plate of pasta on match day, three hours before kick-off. Many, like Beppe Signori, eat a pasta or rice dish at least once a day during the football season. Signori usually eats pasta for lunch and a protein-based dish for dinner, to keep himself at the optimum weight.

Fruit

If pasta is the main superfood, fruit is a close contender. Its high content of water, fibre, sugar, vitamins and minerals makes it an essential part of an athlete's diet.

Fruit should always be eaten ripe when it is easiest to digest and has an optimum nutritional content. Ideally, fruit should also be eaten when it is in season. Avoid fruit that looks past its best – in this state it has very little or no nutritional value.

The exact vitamin and mineral content of fruit varies. Citrus fruits have a high vitamin-C content (100 grams of citrus fruit can provide 40–100 per cent of the total daily requirement). Apricots offer a good supply of vitamin A and potassium. Bananas are also rich in potassium, as well as in phosphorus, natural fibre and sugar. Athletes often choose bananas as they are easy to eat – they do not have a complicated peeling process or too much sticky juice.

Vegetables

Fresh vegetables are excellent sources of many essential nutrients, and the sports superdiet should include plenty of them. To conserve both the flavour and the nutritional value, steam the vegetables, or use the minimum amount of water when boiling them.

Fish

The superdiet includes lots of fresh fish. You should eat fresh white fish as often as possible, and add tuna, anchovies, sardines and mackerel to your diet once or twice a week. Fish tinned in water or brine but *not* oil can occasionally be substituted for fresh fish.

Potentially Harmful Elements in Your Diet

Cholesterol

Raised levels of cholesterol in the blood are linked with coronary heart disease, and saturated fats in the diet can raise levels of blood cholesterol. Animal products are the principal dietary source of saturated fats, particularly offal, eggs, red meat, milk products and some shellfish. A diet high in polyunsaturated and monounsaturated fats, however, is associated with a lower level of blood cholesterol.

Blood cholesterol levels are also influenced by smoking, exercise, weight, temperament and hereditary factors. It is important to keep an eye on your cholesterol levels, and to limit the amount of animal fat in your diet, particularly if there is a history of coronary heart disease in your family.

Coffee

Coffee has no nutritional value. It contains caffeine, which acts as a stimulant. Taken in large amounts, coffee can have a very negative effect on the body, causing the nervous system to overwork, and leading to symptoms such as insomnia and an accelerated heartbeat. In sensible doses, however, it can stimulate the digestive system (which is why it is often drunk after a meal), help combat tiredness, and improve concentration. Italian footballers are permitted a small cup daily. Tea also contains caffeine, but is not a traditional Italian drink. Herbal teas are an excellent alternative to both tea and coffee. Chamomile tea, which has relaxing properties, is a popular drink in Italy.

Chocolate

Chocolate also contains caffeine and acts as a stimulant. Many people enjoy the taste and consistency of chocolate, and it is often the most difficult thing to give up when dieting. Although it is an accessible source of energy, chocolate contains high levels of fat. Within reason, it is not detrimental to the active person's diet.

Alcohol

The Italians generally have a much more balanced view of alcohol than the northern races, who tend to consume it more frequently outside main meals and in larger quantities. Wine is part of the Italian footballers' diet, but generally their attitude towards alcohol is dismissive. Beppe Signori does not mind whether he drinks or not as his philosophy is treating the body with respect and never forgetting that he is an athlete.

Alcohol is absorbed very quickly, entering the bloodstream after 15–30 minutes when drunk on an empty stomach, and in 1–3 hours on a full stomach. The absolute maximum advised amount per week for normal, young, fit, healthy adults is 21 units of alcohol for men, and 14 for women (a unit is equivalent to a small glass of wine or half a pint of beer).

Alcohol should be handled with care – and it is not indispensable for a healthy diet. However, a glass of wine with a meal can aid digestion, stimulate the appetite and help you to relax. Taken in excess, alcohol can cause weight gain as it is high in calories. It can also cause liver disease and problems with the nervous system.

Athletes who overindulge regularly will discover that training becomes harder, their stamina is drastically reduced and they lose interest in their sport as the depressive effects of drink take their toll. Be warned: it is better to drink little or nothing at all than to drink too much. It takes years of hard work to achieve the physique of a top sportsperson, but it takes only a few months to ruin it with alcohol.

Adapting the Diet for Your Needs

The Italian football diet is essentially a healthy diet for life, but you will probably have to adapt it to suit your particular needs. The dietary guidelines featured throughout the book are intended for people participating in active sport at least two or three times a week. Less active people can also follow the diet simply by reducing the calorie intake. Instead of having three courses for lunch and dinner, choose just one course for each meal – a pasta starter for lunch and a protein-based main course dish for dinner, for example. Most fruit and vegetables can be eaten at will, and are an important part of a balanced diet.

The Young Athlete

Athletes up to 18 years of age have slightly different dietary requirements to adults. They generally need more protein as the muscles are still developing. There should also be an increased amount of milk and cheese which contain calcium for growing bones. Both vitamins and minerals are important. The Italian football diet is ideal for young athletes as it is rich in protein, vitamins and minerals.

It is particularly important that adolescent athletes are under medical supervision. As the body is undergoing such enormous change, there must be frequent blood and other chemical checks to ensure that the diet contains the right nutrients.

The Older Athlete

At the other end of the spectrum, the older athlete needs to adapt his or her diet to suit a slightly less demanding exercise routine. The term 'older athlete' applies generally to anyone over the age of 35. Total calorie intake should be reduced by choosing fewer courses, as detailed above, or by eating smaller portions.

2

GETTING FIT

Even top athletes have to work hard at getting fit. Returning from holiday and starting to train again can be agonising at first. This chapter describes how Italian football teams set about regaining fitness, and contains practical suggestions for assessing your fitness levels and adapting the diet and training programme to get you into shape.

For Beppe Signori, the pre-season training is not as difficult as it is for some players as he is an active holiday-maker, swimming and playing tennis whenever possible. Nevertheless, the first few days are hard work and result in many aching muscles. Italian teams usually meet up towards the end of July and disappear to the mountains, either in Italy or in Switzerland, Austria or Germany, to avoid the pulsating heat of inland Italy. Pre-season training usually lasts for three weeks and goes through various phases.

Preparation

The team undergoes various medical checks before setting off for training camp. Doctor Bartolini stresses that such tests are very important for everyone thinking of embarking on rigorous exercise – not just top sportspeople – to ensure they are in good condition. Some teams have special facilities to control various aspects of a player's fitness, including the following tests:

1 Blood – general tests on blood cell counts, and a special look at iron levels, which are particularly important for athletes. Iron is vital in the formation of haemoglobin, the oxygen-carrying constituent of the red blood cells. If the player is anaemic (deficient in iron) he will suffer constant fatigue and be unable to keep up with team mates.

2 Electrocardiogram (ECG) – tests the state of the heart, and its efficiency when the player is at rest or undertaking physical exercise.

3 Bicycle – players pedal on an exercise bicycle while readings of their pulse rate and the level of stress on the heart are taken.

4 Spirometer – measures lung capacity. Heavy smoking decreases lung efficiency, so players are not encouraged to smoke.

5 Eye test – players must have excellent eyesight. They are also tested for colour blindness, as this can have unfortunate consequences during matches.

Although you may not have access to high-tech health-screening facilities, you should see your doctor for a thorough check-up before starting your fitness regime.

Assessing basic fitness

This is important for two main reasons: (1) so that you do not push yourself too hard to begin with, and (2) so that you can monitor your increased level of fitness as you improve during your exercise programme. There are three basic tests for measuring your fitness level.

One-and-a-half mile test

This simply involves running exactly one-and-a-half miles (approximately two-and-a-half km), and measuring the time taken to run the distance. Then consult Figure 2.1 to work out how fit you are.

Point of Maximum Intensity

To find out your basic heart rate, check your pulse before you get out of bed in the morning. The easiest way is to press a finger (not your thumb) lightly against the left side of your neck, just under your chin. Do this for 15 seconds and multiply by 4 to get your heart rate per minute. Take the heart rate again after exercise.

During exercise, your heart rate can reach a level above which you will start to feel drained. This is called the point of maximum intensity. You can

AGE	VERY POOR	POOR	FAIR	GOOD	VERY GOOD	EXCELLENT	SUPERB
Men							
17-29	16:30+	14:30+	12:00+	10:15+	8:15+	7:30+	6:45+
30-34	17:00+	15:00+	12:30+	10:30+	8:30+	7:45+	7:00+
35-39	17:30+	15:30+	13:00+	10:45+	8:45+	8:00+	7:15+
40-44	18:00+	16:00+	13:30+	11:00+	9:00+	8:15+	7:30+
45-49	18:30+	16:30+	14:00+	11:15+	9:15+	8:30+	7:45+
over 50	19:00+	17:00+	14:30+	11:30+	9:30+	8:45+	8:00+
Women							
17-29	19:48+	17:24+	14:24+	12:18+	9:54+	9:00+	8:06+
30-34	20:24+	18:00+	15:00+	12:36+	10:12+	9:18+	8:24+
35-39	21:00+	18:36+	15:36+	12:54+	10:30+	9:36+	8:42+
40-44	21:36+	19:12+	16:12+	13:12+	10:48+	9:54+	9:00+
45-49	22:12+	19:48+	16:48+	13:30+	11:06+	10:30+	9:36+
over 50	22:48+	20:24+	17:24+	13:48+	11:24+	10:30+	9:36+

Figure 2.1. Fitness levels according to time taken to run 1½ miles (2.5 km).

calculate your point of maximum intensity by subtracting your age from 220. You can then use this figure to work out what your heart rate should be at the point of your maximum intensity at which you want to work. If you are unfit, you should exercise at no more than 60 per cent of your maximum intensity. The fitter you are, the higher this percentage can be. Decide on the appropriate percentage then calculate what your heart rate will be at this level by using the Carvonen Formula:

Point of maximum intensity - resting heart rate x chosen percentage + resting heart rate = optimum heart rate during exercise.

Take as an example a reasonably fit, 25-year-old athlete with a resting heart rate of 45 who wants to exercise at 80 per cent of his capabilities. First, the point of maximum intensity is calculated:

220 – 25 = 195

Next, the Carvonen Formula is applied:

195 – 45 x 80% + 45 = 169

The athlete can therefore safely exercise until his heart rate reaches 169.

Physical Activity Index

This is another useful method for monitoring your fitness. Simply make a note of all the exercise sessions you participate in – how often, how intensively and for how long. Then consult Figure 2.2, multiplying the rating for each activity to achieve your score (index = frequency x intensity x time). To be fit enough to embark on the training sessions described in this chapter you should be of at least 'acceptable' fitness. If you are 'sedentary' or 'inactive', you will need to begin a safe exercise programme to increase your fitness levels. A fitness instructor will be able to advise you on the best approach.

Losing Weight

Keeping a constant eye on the scales is a waste of time. Unless weight gain becomes excessive – more than 5 pounds (a couple of kilograms) – emphasis should be placed on how well the athlete feels and whether the diet is satisfying all the nutritional needs.

If, however, you have a tendency to put on too much weight, this will have to be controlled even if you are involved in an active sport. Participating in sport is not a licence to eat what you want, when you want. If anything, you have to be even more careful than less active people, as doing any kind of sporting activity means that the body has to be in optimum condition to cope with the extra demands placed on it. Doctor Bartolini comments 'If a player is very

FREQUENCY	RATING
Daily or almost daily	5
3-5 times per week	4
1-2 times per week	3
Few times per month	2
Less than once a month	1

INTENSITY	
Sustained heavy breathing and perspiration	5
Intermittent heavy breathing and perspiration	4
Moderately heavy	3
Moderate	2
Light	1

TIME	
Over 30 minutes	4
20-30 minutes	3
10-20 minutes	2
Under 10 minutes	1

SCORE	EVALUATION
Under 20	Sedentary
20-40	Inactive
40-60	Acceptable
60-80	Active
100	Very active

Figure 2.2. Physical activity index.

overweight we have to devise not only a diet but also a special individual training programme to help him lose weight as quickly as possible without losing stamina.'

Seven-day Weight-loss Plan

This diet is for an athlete resuming his or her activity after a long rest period who has some weight to lose. It is not for athletes in good condition who have taken a few weeks off (see page 67). The seven-day weight-loss plan, which may be repeated for another week, should be followed in conjunction with daily training sessions of 1½–2 hours' duration. Before you start the diet, you should note the following general guidelines:

- Eliminate the following calorie-laden foods from your diet: fatty and preserved meats, mayonnaise and rich sauces.
- Put the frying pan away. Grill, bake or cook in foil to conserve the essential nutrients. If fried foods are a passion they may be eaten occasionally, and not in abundance.
- Replace sweet, fizzy drinks such as cola with fresh fruit juices, mineral water and herbal teas.
- Sit down for every meal, including snacks.
- Use small plates – a full plate is less likely to make you feel deprived.
- Drink at least 2½–3½ pints (1.5–2 litres) of water a day, outside main meals.
- Eliminate *all* alcohol.

<u>DAY 1</u>

Breakfast

Cup of tea with lemon or semi-skimmed milk, tsp brown sugar or honey
2 wholemeal crackers, thinly spread with jam or honey

Morning Snack

7 oz (200 g) fresh fruit (peaches, apricots, melon)

Lunch

Grated carrot with lemon and salt dressing
3 oz (80 g) spaghetti and tomato sauce with 1 tsp Parmesan cheese
5–7 oz (150–200 g) mixed salad with 2 oz (60 g) soya granules or maize, or 3 oz (80 g) mozzarella balls, dressed with 2 tsps vinaigrette

Afternoon Snack

Glass of unsweetened fruit juice
2 wholemeal biscuits with jam or honey

Dinner

Vegetable soup (without pasta or rice)
5 oz (150 g) thin-sliced tender beef grilled until rare, dressed with lemon juice and salt
7–10½ oz (200–300 g) mixed salad with tomatoes dressed with 2 tsps oil plus salt and herbs
2½ oz (70 g) wholemeal or soya bread

DAY 2

Breakfast

Small carton of low-fat yoghurt mixed with 2 dessertspoons of muesli (or as for Day 1)

Morning Snack

5 oz (140 g) banana *or* glass unsweetened fruit juice (or as for Day 1)

Lunch

3 oz (80 g) pasta with tomato and pea sauce
1 portion runner beans, spinach or uncooked vegetables of your choice dressed with 2 tsps oil
2 balls of lemon or strawberry sorbet *or* 1 portion fresh-fruit salad

Afternoon Snack

7 oz (200 g) fresh fruit *or* glass of tomato or pineapple juice

Dinner

10½ oz (300 g) mashed potato with garlic strips, parsley and 1 tsp vinaigrette *or* 2½ oz (70 g) wholemeal or soya bread
9 oz (250 g) white fish either baked on its own or in a tomato sauce with 2 tsps oil *or* 5 oz (150 g) grilled chicken or turkey breast
Fresh raw or cooked vegetables

<u>DAY 3</u>

Breakfast

As for Days 1 or 2

Morning Snack

Glass of citrus fruit juice, pineapple juice or tomato juice

Lunch

Vegetable minestrone with pasta (or rice) *or* 1 oz (30 g) pasta with 2 oz (60 g) pulses, garnished with herbs
1 portion of cooked vegetables *or* tomato salad
1 slice of apple or jam tart

Afternoon Snack

7 oz (200 g) fresh fruit

Dinner

Grilled vegetables such as aubergines, tomatoes, courgettes and sweet peppers dressed with 2 tsps oil, crushed garlic, lemon juice and a few capers
10½ oz (300 g) potatoes, baked or mashed
5 oz (150 g) grilled chicken or turkey breast *or* chicken quarter or rabbit baked in foil or roasted

DAY 4

Breakfast

As for Days 1 or 2

Morning Snack

Glass of semi-skimmed milk with 1 tsp peppermint syrup *or* glass of soya or almond milk *or* 1 small melon

Lunch

2 oz (60 g) lean proscuitto crudo *or* 3 oz (80 g) bresaola
2½ oz (70 g) wholemeal or soya bread
Vegetables dressed with 2 tsps oil
3½ oz (180 g) light mozzarella cheese

Afternoon Snack

Large slice of fresh pineapple *or* 2 kiwis *or* 1 large peach

Dinner

5–7 oz (150–200 g) gnocchi (potato-based pasta) with tomato sauce and Parmesan cheese *or* 6–7 oz (180–200 g) fresh egg fettucine with bolognese, pesto or tomato and basil sauce
1 portion mixed vegetables dressed with lemon, garlic and parsley *or* spinach or asparagus dressed with lemon juice

DAY 5

Breakfast

As for Days 1 or 2

Morning Snack

7 oz (200 g) fresh fruit

Lunch

3 oz (80 g) pasta with sliced fresh tomatoes, peas or clams
1 large portion mixed salad with 1¾ oz (50 g) fresh tuna or tinned tuna in brine (*not* oil), 1¾ oz grain granules or 2 oz (60 g) maize or soya granules

Afternoon Snack

Fruit ice cream

Dinner

Tomato salad with cucumber and radishes
1 9-oz (250-g) fillet of plaice or sole baked in 2 tsps oil for 10–20 minutes *or* grilled chicken, turkey, rabbit or grilled
1¾ oz (50 g) wholemeal or soya bread
Portion of cooked vegetables

DAY 6

Breakfast

Cup of tea with lemon or milk
2 bran biscuits *or* bowl of bran cereal or muesli with
semi-skimmed milk

Morning Snack

Glass of citrus fruit juice or tomato juice

Lunch

Mixed salad dressed with vinegar or lemon, sea salt
and 1 tsp olive oil
2½ oz (70 g) wholemeal or soya bread

Afternoon Snack

Glass of fruit juice *or* small carton of low-fat yoghurt

Dinner

Portion of raw or cooked vegetables
Small whole Neopolitan or mushroom pizza
Unlimited fresh fruit

DAY 7

Breakfast

Small carton of low-fat yoghurt *or* 5 oz (150 g) fresh fruit (or as for previous days)

Morning Snack

As for previous days

Lunch

5 oz (150 g) ravioli filled with spinach and ricotta cheese with tomato sauce *or* 3 oz (80 g) pasta with bolognese sauce
Vegetables or mixed salad
1 small apple or jam tart *or* 1 portion of ice cream

Afternoon Snack

7 oz (200 g) fresh fruit

Dinner

Vegetable soup (without pasta or rice)
7–9 oz (200–250 g) grilled fresh fish or shellfish *or* chicken kebabs
Mixed salad dressed with 2 tsps oil
1¼ oz (50 g) wholemeal or soya bread

Training

After all the general tests, the team is ready to leave for the mountain retreat. 'This is where the real work starts,' admits Beppe Signori. Most English players who spend time with Italian clubs find the initial training very difficult because they are unused to it.

You may find it useful to compare the following description of the Italian training regime with your own programme. It is full of valuable information on training procedures and on regulating diet and lifestyle for best results. This is followed by an adaptation of the three-week regime for the 'average' sportsperson.

Before you read on, remember that this training programme has been devised for professionals. It is dangerous for any amateur to follow, especially without expert supervision. Beppe Signori comments, 'Don't forget we have trained physios, masseurs, dietitians and doctors at hand to monitor us constantly – and we still get injured.'

Remember, too, that the programme is designed for footballers. Football requires good overall fitness: in the lower body for running and kicking, and in the upper body for throw-ins and heading the ball. You need a good basis of muscular strength as there is quite a lot of jumping and kicking involved (which also requires balance). There are a lot of potential injuries, particularly to the hamstrings and knees, as often not enough precautions are taken. It is useful to spend some time considering the requirements for your particular sport, and what it is that you would like to achieve. In the case of football there are two main physical requirements: (1) sprint and quick recovery, and (2) sustaining the physical intensity. This is also the case for many other sports.

Italian teams usually have three weeks of pre-season training, which is divided into three one-week phases. Training sessions will vary according to the precise needs of each team, and may differ from this version.

Week One

The first week is spent building resistance and speed. This is important for smaller players, like Signori, who profit from their agility and speed, enabling them to turn, unlock the opposition's defence and sprint into the penalty box. During the morning the players go on 45-minute running sessions through the hills. Individual speed training also takes place. This varies according to the player's needs – midfielders run the most, strikers need to sprint fast over short distances, defenders cover quite a lot of ground, and goalkeepers do not need to run much at all.

The afternoon begins with a warm-up session of stretching exercises. This is followed by work on technical skills such as ball control, passing and accuracy.

Week Two

During the second week the cross-country distances are reduced, and the players spend time trying to increase their speeds over 100–200 metres. The afternoon session begins with a warm-up as usual. This may then be followed by a match – either five-a-side or full team – in order to work on tactics. On other days, the players work on ball possession, which also sharpens their reactions and concentration.

Towards the end of the second week, the first full friendly match takes place, usually against the local team, and the players hope they do not show themselves up. This is the team's chance to start hammering home the goals but it does not always happen. Sometimes the manager is experimenting with new tactics or trying out various players in slightly different positions, so the team has to revise its habits as well. Some seasons begin with a new manager at the helm, and the players have to absorb his way of doing things. Being together during this training period is very important for the players as it teaches them to think and act as a team, not just as individuals.

Week Three

The morning training sessions start to resemble those that take place once the season has started: the players still work on speed and running over short distances, but there is also technical work – skills such as ball control and teamwork. Different types of players may have separate sessions – strikers may practise scoring, for example. The afternoons are spent playing full friendly matches, usually against international sides or in tournaments. The players then have a few days off before returning home to resume normal training, and to complete their series of friendly matches.

Training Programme for 'Average' Athletes

The training programme on pages 55–57 has been adapted from the Italian regime for the non-professional. Be sensible – monitor your heart rate as you exercise and do not push yourself beyond your limits. The programme will enable you to achieve increased fitness in all areas, which are prioritised as follows:

1 Aerobic fitness is needed for stamina and for recovering quickly.
2 Flexibility reduces the risk of injury.
3 Strength also reduces the risk of injury and provides a stable base for power work.
4 Agility is important to facilitate particular skills.
5 Anaerobic speed (sprinting) and recovery can be worked on once good levels of speed and strength have been attained.
6 Power can only be developed when there is enough muscular strength and flexibility to reduce the risk of injury.

Preparation

If you have been inactive for a long period, do not start the training programme 'cold'. Spend a week preparing yourself by going for brisk walks and short jogs, gradually increasing the time spent on these activities. The time you take to reach full fitness should be in proportion to the time that has elapsed since you last participated in active sport. Do not expect to bounce right back into full fitness if you have not trained for 10 years. This will only increase the risk of injury. Take up to six weeks to build up activity levels gradually to the point where you can run at a steady pace for 30–35 minutes four times a week.

Take at least one day off each week. When you begin the programme, you should rest every other day. Every four weeks, have an 'easy' week where you do not push yourself so hard to allow the body to adapt to increased levels of activity.

Preventing Injury

It is vital to warm-up before every exercise session. Wearing a tracksuit to keep you warm, carry out easy, rhythmic movements using your arms and legs, such as walking, skipping and light jogging. Warming-up is particularly important before anaerobic exercise, such as sprinting or jumping. Structure the warm-up to give you enough mobility. Start with small movements, gradually increasing the stretch or speed, depending on the movement. Stretch regularly, a little every day, and always after exercise, and 'warm down' before finishing each session by sitting down and carrying out slow, relaxing stretches.

Running or exercising on unsuitable surfaces can cause injury, so if in doubt, stick to grass. Power and strength exercises – such as jumping on the spot and kicking out – carry a greater risk of injury and should be done only once a week. Allow a longer recovery time at this stage, decreasing it gradually.

Running

Jogging should be done at a comfortable pace, but run at a fast pace that is sustainable but challenging. Never increase your running time or distance by more than 20 per cent each week, and build up running distance before concentrating on speed. Gradually add bursts of speed over a distance that is relevant to your sport.

Two terms are used in the training programme that may be unfamiliar to you: 'fartlek' is a steady run interspersed with bursts of speed; 'intervals' is a sprint session followed by recovery then repeats.

Building Fitness

Flexibility

All athletes need to be flexible. The Italian fitness programme involves both dynamic and static exercises for flexibility. Static flexibility work e.g. moving straight into a full stretch with no gradual preceding movement, must be done in the presence of an experienced instructor. Flexibility exercises should be done after the general activity when the body has fully warmed up. Include balancing exercises when working on flexibility, such as hopping on the spot.

Agility

Exercises for agility include running forwards, backwards, sideways, turning and negotiating obstacles. Another approach is the 'step square', which involves standing in the middle of a special square block, and following the commands of your instructor to jump forwards, backwards, right or left. Sometimes a hexagonal step is used to make the exercise even more challenging.

Strength

Many exercises can improve strength, including:

- step-ups
- squats
- lunges
- abdominal curls (lying on your back with knees bent and lifting shoulders off the floor towards the shoulders)
- press-ups
- hip flexions (hanging from bar and raising knees, or sitting on the edge of a chair, with your hands supporting your back, bringing your knees in quickly and releasing them slowly)

Power

Work on muscular strength and endurance before developing power to avoid injury. Hopping, skipping, bounding, jumping, throw-ins and work with a medicine ball (heavy leather ball) can all improve power. The medicine ball is good for strengthening elastic recall – drawing the ball back before throwing instead of throwing from a static position.

Stretching

Dynamic stretching exercises involve moving in stages towards a full stretch, pausing and holding the stretch at each stage. Static stretching exercises, on the other hand, mean moving straight into a full stretch, and as already mentioned, must be done in the presence of an expert. You should stretch for at least 15 minutes every day, but this can be broken up into several short sessions.

Guidelines

1 Start the programme nine weeks before the season for your sport commences.
2 Follow the programme through to week six.
3 Repeat weeks four, five and six.
4 When you move into the playing phase, follow the maintenance programme (see page 61).
5 If you have to take a break due to illness or injury, resume your training programme a little further back than the place you left off.

6 Eat well – follow the training diet.

7 Monitor your heart rate throughout the exercise programme, especially during the first few days. Do not exercise beyond your point of maximum intensity (see page 33).

8 Be very careful not to injure the lower spine – support it as much as possible during exercise.

9 Allow yourself sufficient recovery time during exercise. You can calculate your recovery time by timing how long it takes for your heart beat to return to normal after it has reached the point of maximum intensity. The fitter you are, the shorter your recovery time will be.

10 Work in pairs for some of the exercises as it adds strength.

11 From Week 4 onwards, start to include more sessions of skill rehearsal and match play.

12 Exercise times are not given for strength, power and agility sessions because they vary according to individual capabilities. Ideally, these exercises should initially be carried out under professional supervision.

WEEK 1	EXERCISE	DURATION (MINUTES)
Monday	Warm-up	15
	Stretching	15
Tuesday	Warm-up	15
	Stretching	15
Wednesday	Warm-up	15
	Stretching	15
Thursday	Warm-up	15
	Strength work	
	Stretching	15
Friday	Warm-up	15
	Stretching	15
Saturday	Warm-up	15
	Agility (and ball) work	
	Stretching	15
Sunday	Rest day	
WEEK 2		
Monday	Warm-up	20
	Stretching	15
Tuesday	Warm-up	15
	Stretching	15
Wednesday	Warm-up	15
	Stretching	15
Thursday	Warm-up	20
	Strength work	
	Stretching	15
Friday	Warm-up	2
	Stretching	15
	Agility and strength work	
Saturday	Warm-up	25
	Agility and strength work	
	Stretching	15
Sunday	Rest day	
WEEK 3		
Monday	Warm-up	30
	Stretching	15

Tuesday	Warm-up	15
	Running	15
	Stretching	15
Wednesday	Warm-up	20
	Stretching	15
Thursday	Warm up	20
	Strength work	
	Stretching	15
Friday	Warm-up	20
	Stretching	15
Sunday	Rest day	

WEEK 4

Monday	Warm-up	20
	Stretching	15
Tuesday	Warm-up	15
	Stretching	15
Wednesday	Warm-up	15
	Running	15
	Stretching	15
Thursday	Warm-up	15
	Strength work	
	Stretching	15
Friday	Warm-up	15
	Stretching	15
Saturday	Warm-up	20
	Agility (and ball) work	
	Stretching	15
Sunday	Rest day	

WEEK 5

Monday	Warm-up	15
	Intervals (see page 000)	30
	Stretching	15
Tuesday	Warm-up	15
	Agility (and ball) work	
	Stretching	15
Wednesday	Warm-up	35
	Stretching	15

Thursday	Warm-up	20
	Strength and power work	
	Stretching	15
Friday	Warm-up	20
	Stretching	15
Saturday	Warm-up	15
	Running	15
	Agility and strength work	
	Stretching	15
Sunday	Rest day	

WEEK 6

Monday	Warm-up	15
	Fartlek (see page 000)	40
Tuesday	Warm-up	15
	Stretching	15
Wednesday	Warm-up	15
	Intervals	15
	Stretching	15
Thursday	Warm-up	25
	Strength and power work	
	Stretching	15
Friday	Warm-up	35
	Stretching	15
Saturday	Warm-up	20
	Agility and strength work	
	Stretching	15
Sunday	Rest day	

Figure 2.3. Six-week training schedule for the average athlete.

Training Diet

The pre-season training diet is very important. After the summer holidays the body will not be in prime condition, so as well as the heavy training sessions there must be the right dietary balance.

There are a few general rules for the pre-season diet. As they are based on the needs of footballers, do not worry if the training routine for your sport does not allow for such a regime. Follow the rules as closely as you can, but adapt them to your particular needs. For suitable recipes, see Chapter 5.

1 Breakfast must be eaten two hours before training. Build up your glycogen reserves by eating starchy foods such as breakfast cereal, toast or wholemeal crackers.

2 Lunch must be eaten three hours before training or a match.

3 At every lunch and dinner you must add:
(i) an antipasto (starter) of fresh vegetables. Experiment with salads using fresh, high-quality ingredients, such as tomato and basil; mixed greens; radicchio; fennel, celery and carrot; French carrots (grated carrot dressed with oil, salt and lemon juice); rocket with raw mushrooms; cucumber and tomato.
(ii) at least ½ pint (0.25 litre) of still or lightly sparkling mineral water.

(iii) 1¼ ounces (50 grams) of bread, crackers or grissini, to be eaten after the antipasto or first dish.

4   You are allowed one glass of wine or beer during dinner only.

5   You are allowed to have a cup of coffee or tea at the end of lunch or dinner.

6   A main course may be substituted by a vegetable dish with a sauce on it.

7   Recipes within the same food group are interchangeable. The four basic groups are: cereal foods and starchy vegetables; fruit and vegetables; meat and alternatives; milk and milk products.

8   When choosing the main dish you must maintain a balanced diet by remembering the following:

(i)   eat meat and fish four times a week.

(ii) eat cheese three times a week.

(iii) eat egg dishes twice a week.

9   You may eat one dessert a day, at either lunch or dinner (see Chapter 5 for suggestions).

10 Snacks should be eaten twice a day. Choose either fresh fruit (7 oz/200 g) or a fruit salad. After training, choose carbohydrate snacks – the body needs at least 1¼ oz (50 g) of carbohydrate in the two hours after a training session.

11 Lost mineral salts must be replaced after every training session. In Italy, doctors recommend packets of mineral salts to add to a glass of water and drink after each session. In the UK, sports drinks and food are used to replace minerals.

Banned Foods

The following foods are not allowed in the diet because they are high in fat and calories, and can be difficult to digest.

- full cream milk
- eels
- salmon
- processed and pre-packaged foods (high in additives)
- crisps
- pickles and sauces
- dressings (unless otherwise specified)
- all preserved meat except for cooked and raw ham (proscuitto) and bresaola
- full-fat cheese or fermented cheese (soft cream cheese, Gruyère and others of a similar nature)
- figs, dried fruit
- fruit in syrup
- chestnuts
- spirits

3

STAYING FIT

Now you are fit you have to work at it to stay that way. You may now be playing your chosen sport regularly, but this is not enough. A maintenance training programme and diet are essential if you want to keep in top shape.

Maintenance Training

Once the football season is under way, the Italian team follows a regular training schedule. Their typical week is spent in careful preparation for the forthcoming match. It involves frequent exercise and practice sessions, but important relaxation periods are also built in. The following summary of the players' typical week will give you some idea of what is involved in maintaining optimum fitness and performance.

A Week in the Life of a Serie A Team

Sunday

Match day.

Monday

A much-needed day off for the team members who played on Sunday. The reserves who did not get a game go to the training ground for some light training. Injured players also go in for treatment.

Tuesday

Training starts again, either in the morning or the afternoon, depending on the manager's preference. There is a warm-up session, then some stretching and general exercises to keep the body supple. The 22 players in the first-team squad then divide into two teams for a match, which tends to last for around 30 minutes.

Wednesday

There are generally two training sessions, one in the morning and one in the afternoon. The morning session consists of athletic exercises, such as repetitive runs of 200–300 metres on the pitch, followed by work in the gym on parts of the body that may need strengthening. The afternoon is spent playing a match in which speed, working on ball-possession and reading the game are emphasised.

Thursday

There is usually only one session, which consists of either normal training exercises or a friendly match played locally.

Friday

In an afternoon session, the players perform stretching exercises, working particularly on the spine, and also spend time on individual techniques. The squad then divides up for a match, during which the manager works out the final team tactics, and usually decides who will play in Sunday's match.

Saturday

In the morning the team gathers for a final training session. This consists of a warm-up, speed work and a short match of approximately 20 minutes. Then it is off to the team hotel unless, like AC Milan, the club has overnight facilities for the squad.

This overnight stay is vitally important for team morale. All players must stay unless they have family problems or are too ill to play in the match. The team use this as valuable preparation time, watching videos of the opposing team, and discussing tactics. It also gives them time to socialise and build up a rapport by eating and relaxing together, and going out to the cinema on Saturday afternoon. This approach is in marked contrast to the pre-match preparation of English teams, who rarely spend the evening together before a match. The Italians will sometimes spend several days in a hotel if the team is on a losing streak, or faces a particularly important match.

Fitness Tips

While you are playing your sport regularly, carrying out the following training exercises will help you to give your best performance consistently:

- one long running session a week
- one session of sprinting per week
- at least one strength/power/agility session per week (see Chapter Two)
- daily stretching exercises

Maintenance Diet

The principles of eating a balanced, nutritious diet are the same for the maintenance diet as for the pre-season training diet detailed in Chapter 2. The only difference is that you need to reduce the number of calories. This is because training sessions should not be as tough as they were when you were fighting to get back into shape.

Like most Italian players, Beppe Signori knows that his lifestyle, especially his diet, is of paramount importance. A sensible diet has become part of his life. Being a small, quick striker he immediately feels any weight gain and controls it by cutting down on the amount he eats, but he never misses a meal. Dr Bartolini comments, 'Our players keep to their optimum weight by eating well and being happy. A miserable player who is always watching what he eats is no good in a competitive sport where morale is a very important factor.' If you suddenly start to put on or lose weight for no obvious reason, see your doctor as there may be an underlying medical reason.

To help you reduce your calorie intake simply follow these guidelines:

1 Regulate your meals according to your body's needs.
2 Eliminate puddings and sweet dishes, but allow yourself the occasional treat.
3 Eat only a main course at each meal.
4 If you combine pasta with protein, eat a smaller than usual amount of either.
5 If you choose to eat a rich pasta meal on a particular day, keep the protein course light at the other main meal of the day, for example a caprese, which is a mozzarella and tomato salad.

Following the maintenance diet not only provides you with the nutrients you need, it is also fun. As Dr Bartolini comments, 'A diet for physically active people is not meant to be a torture.' Treat yourself occasionally. Do not be too rigid about the diet or it will become boring and make you unhappy. Enjoy the delicious recipes in Chapter 5 – the plates of pasta with natural foods and delicious sauces. And remember that the aim of the diet is to make you feel well, and to give your body what it needs to cope with your active lifestyle. Finally, relax and enjoy yourself.

Match-day Diet

When the big day arrives, the players follow a special match-day diet. If you are preparing to compete in your sport, then observe these rules:

1 Eat starchy food for breakfast to build up your glycogen reserves (see page 12).

2 Eat lunch at least three hours before the match. Lunch should consist of:

(i) ½ pint (¼ litre) still or lightly sparkling mineral water

(ii) a large portion of pasta (4–5 oz/120–150 g) with a light sauce (tomato and basil with a little parmesan cheese, or oil, lemon and parmesan cheese)

(iii) ¼–1 oz (20–30 g) proscuitto crudo or bresaola

3 Just before the match eat one or two spoons of honey, which provides sustained energy. If it is a hot and humid day, take a dose of integrated salts diluted in lots of water to prevent cramp.

4 Just after the match eat a large portion of starchy food to refuel your energy supply, and drink another dose of diluted integrated salts.

5 Dinner should consist of the following

(i) an antipasto of fresh vegetables

(ii) 4–5 oz (120–150 g) of pasta with sauce of your choice

(iii) a portion of simply cooked vegetables or a vegetable dish from the recipe section

(iv) half a portion of a fish or meat main course with sauce of your choice

(v) 50 g of white or wholemeal bread, grissini or crackers

(vi) ½ pint (¼ litre) of still or lightly sparkling mineral water.

Holiday Fitness

When the sporting season is over it is tempting to let your diet and fitness regime slip. A holiday is a valuable period in which to restore your mental and physical resources after a busy year and generally take time out to enjoy yourself. There is, however, a danger in becoming too undisciplined – lazing by the pool all day, eating plates of junk food and drinking too much alcohol.

Claudio Bartolini is realistic and cautionary about the holiday period. He explains that the Serie A training diet is so appetising and rewarding that many players do not want to drop it once the holiday period comes around.

Beppe Signori does not throw the diet book out of the window when he goes on holiday, but he enjoys some good home cooking when he goes to visit his mother. Even though he enjoys sitting on the beach and soaking up the sun, he also remains very active by swimming and playing tennis. Many of his team mates have a similar philosophy and engage in alternative sports when on holiday. This means that most of them return to start pre-season training in good condition.

It is unwise to pile on too many pounds, not only because they are difficult to lose, but also because the weight puts a strain on the body when the tough pre-season training starts. When you are aged 18 or 19 it is quite easy to lose excess weight, but after 25 it becomes more difficult, and your body becomes less able to adjust to huge swings of either weight and/or general fitness. The age barriers are being pushed back constantly – athletes like Linford Christie have proved that you can win and be at the top of your profession well into your 30s. But it takes hard work and discipline. If you do not respect your body then you cannot expect it to carry on competing at a top level for many years.

As well as eating healthily on holiday, take advantage of the sunshine and fresh air to enjoy a few weeks with friends or family. The pressures of work can adversely affect relationships, especially if you are involved in a demanding sport during your free time.

Holidays are an opportunity to spend time building them up again and enjoying the company of those closest to you. As this diet is so flexible, you can involve the whole family – even children will love the pasta and delicious sauces. And why not try out some of your own recipes during the holidays?

You can enjoy your holiday time to the full, and return to your sport in reasonably good shape simply by following a few guidelines:

1 Continue to eat plenty of fresh fruit and vegetables, ensuring they are washed well and in good condition.

2 Supplement your diet with vitamins if the fruit and vegetables are not up to standard.

3 Drink plenty of liquids, particularly if visiting hot climates, but avoid ice and drinking the local water if you are at all dubious about it.

4 When visiting a country where Mediterranean-style food is difficult to find, pick the simplest and most wholesome choices on the menu.

5 Choose fresh, high-quality meat and fish.

6 Drink more alcohol and enjoy yourself but do not allow yourself to become dehydrated.

7 If you do 'pig out' for a couple of days, spend a day eating only fresh fruit and drinking water to 'detoxify'.

8 Do not skip meals and allow your routine to get completely out of control.

9   Unless you feel noticeably heavier do not weigh yourself. Weight can fluctuate for a number of reasons, such as jet lag, and changes of diet and routine.

10 Keep active – do some 'holiday' sport you enjoy.

11 Relax and enjoy yourself.

4

SPECIAL NEEDS

Like everyone else, athletes get ill from time to time. They are also at risk from injury – from sprains and strains to torn muscles and broken bones. Most people accept that a doctor's guidance is called for when an athlete falls ill, but now it seems that diet can also help.

Claudio Bartolini has had enormous experience in this field, first as an active sportsman, then as a sports doctor. For nearly 20 years he has been responsible for the mental and physical wellbeing of the athletes in his care. He believes that it is his duty to be 'in contact with the best medical teams in the world'. If one of his players has a serious problem he feels he should know who the expert is in that field, and where he or she is located. He was in constant contact with top London surgeon John Browett during Paul Gascoigne's recovery from his serious knee injury, and was recently following Thomas Doll's progress when he had intensive treatment on a knee injury in his native Germany. Being up to date and well informed is an important part of his job.

Doctor Bartolini believes that it is always best to listen to medical advice when you are ill or injured. You may think you know your body better than anyone else, but the doctors understand the type of injury and how long it may take to heal. Some injuries, such as muscle strain and torn ligaments, may feel as if they have cleared up, but can actually take a long time to get back to normal. Never try to force recovery. Returning to competitive activity too soon after an illness or injury can cause a more serious injury or set-back, leading to a longer lay off.

The players have a complete physical examination twice a year, and basic blood and urine analysis every 45 days. Players with weight problems are seen by the doctor up to two times a week to monitor their weight and try to find out what is causing the problem. They have to give full accounts of what and when they have eaten and drunk.

Women Athletes

Iron levels can drop during menstruation, so it is wise to increase the intake of red meat, green vegetables and pulses. Iron is less easily absorbed from vegetable sources than from meat, but can be improved by consuming food or drinks rich in vitamin C at the same time. Iron-enriched breakfast cereal with a glass of orange juice is a good combination. Following the Serie A diet and drinking plenty of fluids is good general advice, but if you have any specific problems with menstruation, see your doctor.

If you are pregnant, your doctor will advise you about modifying your diet and taking additional vitamin and mineral supplements.

Colds and Flu

When an athlete is suffering from a heavy cold or bout of 'flu, it is important to pay special attention to the diet. A fever will increase the amount of energy expended and also reduce the appetite, two things which cause loss of weight. The following guidelines can help:

1   Drink plenty of fluids.
2   Eat small meals frequently to try and maintain the intake of necessary nutrients.
3   Stick to appetising and easily digested food with light sauces. Pasta is ideal. Try Pasta with Vegetables (see page 89) or Pasta and Pulses (see page 99). Fish is excellent and easily digestible, especially steamed or baked.
4   If you are unable to eat, ask your doctor to recommend one of the special nutritionally enriched drinks available.

5 Sweet things may be more attractive. Drink fruit juices, add honey to other drinks, and see if cakes or pies stimulate your appetite, but be sensible – do not neglect your overall balanced diet.

6 To get the right intake of calcium and easily digested protein, add yoghurt, milk shakes, egg dishes and meringue to your diet.

7 If your mouth and throat are dry, use a mouthwash frequently to ensure there is no bad taste in the mouth which could put you off food.

Inactivity

Any period of inactivity is a problem for an athlete. The injury or illness itself needs to be overcome, which takes time, and the missed training means that the athlete needs to get fit again.

After a long lay-off – a serious knee injury for example – it is necessary to work on the knee but also on the surrounding muscles. After the knee has healed, there may be all kinds of muscle strains as the body tries to regain full fitness, so it is essential to progress slowly and follow the advice of a specialist.

Broken Bones

The following rules are essential for optimum recovery:

1 Increase the daily intake of calcium, which is vital in bone formation.
2 Reduce calorie intake as less energy is needed while you are inactive.
3 Continue to eat fresh fruit and vegetables at will, which provide necessary vitamins and minerals.
4 See a physiotherapist. You must begin to use your damaged limb to avoid weakening of the bone and muscle.
5 Drink at least 3½–5 pints (2–3 litres) of liquid a day to flush out the kidneys and help prevent the formation of stones.
6 Supplement the diet with daily doses of vitamin C and a multivitamin tablet, especially in winter.

RECIPES

This chapter contains a wealth of recipes for delicious, satisfying and healthy meals, all of which are regularly enjoyed by Serie A footballers. Specialist ingredients should be widely available from Italian delicatessens. Recipes give quantities for four servings. The approximate calorie content of each recipe per portion is also indicated:

- Low-calorie dishes contain fewer than 300 calories
- Medium-calorie dishes contain between 300 and 500 calories
- High-calorie dishes contain more than 500 calories.

This information will make it easy for you to plan your meals according to the dietary guidelines in the previous chapters. The only problem you are likely to have is being spoilt for choice.

Cooking techniques

Before you start, bear in mind that to get the most out of a recipe, the food should be prepared in a way that best preserves its nutritional value. Following these guidelines may help:

1 Vegetables should be cooked by boiling in a minimum amount of water to preserve their vitamins and minerals. Vegetables boiled in a lot of water can lose up to 80 per cent of their nutrients. Keep any cooking water for sauces, soups and minestrones. Depending on the exact method, steaming can also be a good way to promote nutrient retention.

2 Cook fruit and vegetables whole if possible, as more nutrients are lost when the food is cut.

3 Pasta, the sports superfood, should always be cooked *al dente* – just firm with some resistance when bitten. For the quantities of pasta specified in the following recipes, use 7 pints (4 litres) of cooking water. This is only a guide – pasta can be cooked in much less water. Add salt to the water if you like, but this should be a matter of personal preference. Cook dried pasta according to the packet instructions, usually for 10–12 minutes; fresh pasta needs only about 5 minutes cooking time.

4 Rice should always be tender and well cooked.

5 Pulses should be soaked overnight, drained and boiled in fresh, unsalted water for 10 minutes, then simmered until tender. Adding salt hardens the pulses – this is especially true of beans rather than lentils.

6 Do not add unnecessary fat to food when roasting or baking.

7 Use very hot oil for frying to prevent too much being absorbed by the food.

8 Microwave cooking is another good way to retain nutritional value in vegetables. It is not, however, a popular method in Italy as many traditional dishes simply are not adapted to this method, and Italian cooks enjoy the rituals of conventional cooking.

9 When using frozen foods, follow packet instructions carefully. Never refreeze thawed food. You cannot freeze salads, hard-boiled eggs, uncooked potatoes or mayonnaise.

10 Always use fresh ingredients and food of the highest quality. Tired salads and badly stored fruit have little nutritional value.

11 Sea salt or salt substitute may be used where salt is indicated.

Pasta Dishes

PASTA IN CLASSIC TOMATO SAUCE
MEDIUM-CALORIE DISH

Ingredients
11 oz (320 g) pasta of your choice
2 teaspoons olive oil
1 clove garlic, crushed
½ small onion, finely chopped
½ stick celery, finely chopped
½ carrot, finely chopped
1 18-oz (500-g) carton passata or 1½ lb (675 g) very
ripe plum tomatoes, peeled and liquidised
3–4 basil leaves

OPTIONAL
3½ oz (100 g) garden peas
5 oz (150 g) mussels or clams, prepared
7 oz (200 g) mushrooms, finely chopped
¼ pepper, cut into strips and finely chopped
½ aubergine, diced
2–3 canned artichoke hearts, finely chopped
5–7 oz (150–200 g) asparagus tips

Method

1 Cook the pasta so it is ready when the sauce is cooked.

2 Gently heat the oil in a non-stick saucepan and fry the garlic and onion until softened.

3 Add the celery and carrot and cook for a few minutes.

4 Stir in the passata or tomatoes and continue to cook over a low heat for about 15–20 minutes, stirring occasionally. Add a little water if the sauce becomes too thick.

5 Drain the pasta and add it to the sauce, mixing well before pouring into a serving dish and garnishing with a few basil leaves.

6 For variation, add one of the optional ingredients to the sauce after cooking the garlic and onion and before adding the tomatoes.

MACARONI IN RED SAUCE

MEDIUM-CALORIE DISH

Ingredients

11 oz (320 g) macaroni
2 tablespoons olive oil
1 small onion, finely chopped
1 small carrot, finely chopped
1 stick celery, finely chopped
1 14-oz (400-g) tin chopped tomatoes
salt
½ oz (15 g) butter
2 tablespoons flour
7 fl oz (200 ml) semi-skimmed milk
3 tablespoons grated Parmesan cheese

Method

1 Cook the pasta so it is ready when the sauce is cooked.

2 Heat the oil in a saucepan. Add the onion, carrot and celery, and cook gently for 10 minutes. Stir in the tomatoes and a pinch of salt and leave to cook for 20 minutes, stirring occasionally.

3 Melt the butter in another saucepan, then add the flour and cook for 2 minutes. Stir in the milk and bring the sauce to the boil, stirring all the time until smooth and thickened. Stir in to the tomato sauce.

4 Drain the pasta, then place in a serving dish. Add the sauce and the grated Parmesan cheese. Stir well and serve hot.

PASTA AND LENTILS

MEDIUM-CALORIE DISH

Ingredients

6 oz (170 g) green or brown lentils
2 vegetable stock cubes
1 tablespoon tomato purée
7 oz (200 g) small pasta shapes
2 tablespoons olive oil
1 onion, finely chopped
2 sprigs parsley, finely chopped

Method

1 Cook the lentils in 2 pints (1.25 litres) simmering water, adding the stock cubes and the tomato purée. Allow 30–35 minutes, until tender.

2 Add the pasta and cook for a further 15 minutes, until tender. Then turn off the heat.

3 Meanwhile, heat the oil in a saucepan and gently cook the onion until softened.

4 Add the onion and parsley to the lentils and pasta and serve hot.

MACARONI WITH COUNTRY SAUCE

MEDIUM-CALORIE DISH

Ingredients

11 oz (320 g) macaroni or other short pasta shapes

2 tablespoons olive oil

1 small onion, finely chopped

10 oz (300 g) fresh (uncooked) Italian sausage,

skinned and cut into pieces *

4–5 sage leaves, shredded

1 pinch crushed dried red chillies

salt

½ pint (150 ml) dry white wine

5 oz (150 g) tinned chopped tomatoes

4 oz (120 g) frozen peas

2 tablespoons grated Parmesan cheese

* *Fresh Italian sausages, such as cotechino, are available from delicatessens and specialist shops. They are meaty, coarse textured and full flavoured. If Italian sausage is not available, substitute good-quality, lightly flavoured sausages, such as Cumberland.*

Method

1 Cook the pasta so it is ready when the sauce is cooked.

2 Heat the oil in a medium saucepan and gently soften the onion. Add the sausage, sage and dried chilli and season with salt. Cook, stirring, for about 20 minutes, or until the sausage is cooked.

3 Stir in the wine and leave to evaporate over a high heat. Add the chopped tomatoes and peas, and cook over a medium heat for 5 minutes.

4 When the pasta is cooked, drain and place in a serving dish. Pour on the sauce and sprinkle with the grated Parmesan.

5 Mix well and serve hot.

PASTA WITH SARDINES
MEDIUM-CALORIE DISH

Ingredients
11 oz (320 g) macaroni or other short pasta shapes
4 fresh sardines
2 tablespoons olive oil
1 medium onion, finely chopped
1 1¼-oz (50-g) tin anchovy fillets in oil
1 14-oz (400-g) tin chopped tomatoes
black pepper to taste

Method
1 Cook the pasta so it is ready when the sauce is cooked.

2 Remove the head, backbone and innards from the sardines. Wash well and dry on kitchen paper.

3 Heat the oil in a saucepan and gently cook the onion until softened. Drain, rinse and chop and add to the onion, stirring well.

4 Lower the heat and add the sardines, turning them to ensure both sides are cooked. Cover with the tomatoes and leave to cook for 20 minutes, stirring occasionally.

5 Drain the pasta, place in a serving dish, spoon over the sauce and add pepper to taste.

6 Mix well and serve hot.

PASTA WITH ARTICHOKES

MEDIUM-CALORIE DISH

Ingredients

11 oz (320 g) penne

2 tablespoons olive oil

2 cloves garlic, crushed

¾ oz (20 g) bacon, diced

1 14-oz (400-g) tin artichoke hearts, drained

8 oz (230 g) tomatoes, peeled and chopped

salt and black pepper to taste

1 sprig parsley, chopped

Method

1 Cook the pasta so it is ready when the sauce is cooked.

2 Heat the oil in a saucepan and gently brown the garlic. Cook the bacon with the garlic for a few minutes then add the artichoke hearts.

3 Mix in the chopped tomatoes and season with salt. Cover the pan and leave to cook over a low heat for 25 minutes, stirring occasionally.

4 Drain the pasta, place in a serving dish and pour over the sauce. Sprinkle with the chopped parsley and add black pepper to taste.

5 Mix well and serve hot.

PASTA WITH AUBERGINES

MEDIUM-CALORIE DISH

Ingredients

1 large aubergine
salt and black pepper to taste
11 oz (320 g) penne
¼ pint (150 ml) olive oil
4 drained, tinned anchovy fillets, rinsed and chopped
1 clove garlic, crushed
3 tablespoons tinned chopped tomatoes
4 basil leaves, shredded

Method

1 Cut the aubergine into short strips about ½ inch (1 cm) wide. Place in a colander and sprinkle with salt. Leave to stand over a plate for about 30 minutes, then rinse well and dry.

2 Cook the pasta so it is ready when the sauce is cooked.

3 Heat the oil in a saucepan, keeping 2 tablespoons aside, and fry the aubergine until lightly cooked. Place on kitchen paper to absorb excess oil, and keep warm.

4 Add the remaining oil to the pan and gently cook the anchovy fillets and garlic.

5 Stir in the tomatoes, cover and cook for 20 minutes over a low heat, stirring occasionally.

6 Drain the pasta and place in a serving dish. Add the aubergine strips, the sauce and the basil and season with black pepper. Mix well and serve.

TASTY PASTA

MEDIUM-CALORIE DISH

Ingredients

11 oz (320 g) penne
2 tablespoons olive oil
1 medium-sized onion, finely chopped
1 clove garlic, chopped
1 14-oz (400-g) tin chopped tomatoes
salt
1 sprig parsley, chopped
1 sprig rosemary, chopped
1 sage leaf, shredded
4–5 basil leaves, shredded
1 pinch crushed dried red chillies
2 tablespoons grated Parmesan cheese

Method

1 Cook the pasta so it is ready when the sauce is cooked.
2 Heat the oil in a saucepan and gently cook the onion and garlic.
3 Add the tomatoes. Season and simmer for 20 minutes, stirring occasionally.
4 Drain the pasta and add to the sauce. Stir in the herbs, chilli and cheese and cook over a high heat, mixing constantly, for a couple of minutes. Serve immediately.

PASTA WITH VEGETABLES

MEDIUM-CALORIE DISH

Ingredients

11 oz (320 g) rigatoni
4 tablespoons olive oil
1 small onion, finely chopped
1 small aubergine, cut into cubes
1 medium-sized red pepper, sliced
1 medium-sized yellow pepper, sliced
1 medium-sized green pepper, sliced
1 medium-sized courgette, cut into cubes
1 14-oz (400-g) tin chopped tomatoes
1 pinch crushed dried red chillies
4 basil leaves, shredded
2 tablespoons grated Parmesan cheese

Method

1 Cook the pasta so it is ready when the sauce is cooked.

2 Heat the oil in a large pan and cook the onion until softened. Add the aubergine and peppers and cook for a few minutes, stirring. Add the courgette and cook for a further 2 minutes.

3 Stir in the tomatoes and chilli. Season and leave to cook over a medium heat for 20 minutes, stirring occasionally.

4 Drain the pasta and add to the sauce. Stir in the basil and cheese and cook over a high heat for a couple of minutes. Serve hot.

89

PASTA WITH MUSHROOMS AND PEPPERS

MEDIUM-CALORIE DISH

Ingredients

3½ oz (100 g) button mushrooms
11 oz (320 g) sedanini or small rigatoni
3 tablespoons olive oil
1 clove garlic, chopped
1 medium-sized onion, chopped
1 sprig parsley, chopped
1 medium-sized red pepper, chopped
1 medium-sized yellow pepper, chopped
1 medium-sized green pepper, chopped
4 tomatoes, peeled and finely chopped
salt and black pepper to taste
2 tablespoons grated Parmesan cheese

Method

1 De-stalk, wash and slice the mushrooms.
2 Cook the pasta so it is ready when the sauce is cooked.
3 Heat the oil in a large pan and gently cook the garlic, onion and parsley for 5 minutes. Add the mushrooms and peppers and cook for a further 5 minutes. Stir in the tomatoes and cook over a low heat for 5–10 minutes, adding a little water if necessary.
4 Drain the pasta and add to the sauce. Season, then cook over a high heat for 2 minutes, mixing well.
5 Sprinkle with the grated cheese and serve.

PASTA WITH TOMATO AND OREGANO SAUCE

MEDIUM-CALORIE DISH

Ingredients

11 oz (320 g) sedanini or small rigatoni
2 tablespoons olive oil
½ oz (15 g) butter
1 medium-sized onion, finely chopped
7 oz (200 g) tomatoes, peeled and chopped
1 teaspoon dried oregano
salt and black pepper to taste
5 oz (150 g) mozzarella cheese, cubed
1 tablespoon grated Parmesan cheese

Method

1 Cook the pasta so it is ready when the sauce is cooked.

2 Heat the oil and butter in a pan. Add the onion and cook until lightly softened, then stir in the tomatoes and oregano. Season and leave to cook over a medium heat for 10–15 minutes, stirring occasionally.

3 Drain the pasta and add to the sauce. Stir in the mozzarella and Parmesan, mixing constantly for a couple of minutes.

4 When the cheese starts to melt, remove the pan from the heat and serve. Season with black pepper.

SPAGHETTI WITH ANCHOVY

HIGH-CALORIE DISH

Ingredients

11 oz (320 g) spaghetti
4 drained, tinned anchovy fillets
1 14-oz (400-g) tin peeled tomatoes
4 tablespoons olive oil
1 clove garlic, chopped
2 tablespoons grated Parmesan cheese
black pepper to taste

Method

1 Cook the pasta so it is ready when the sauce is cooked.

2 Rinse, dry and chop the anchovy fillets.

3 Drain the tomatoes. Cut into slices, discarding the seeds, and put in a saucepan to heat through.

4 Heat the oil in a separate pan and cook the anchovy with the garlic until soft.

5 Drain the pasta and add to the tomatoes. Stir in the Parmesan cheese, black pepper and anchovy mixture. Stir well and serve hot.

SPAGHETTI WITH AUBERGINE

MEDIUM-CALORIE DISH

Ingredients

11 oz (320 g) spaghetti
3 tablespoons olive oil
1 clove garlic, finely chopped
1 aubergine, cut into cubes
1 14-oz (400-g) tin chopped tomatoes
salt and black pepper to taste
1¼ oz (50 g) firm ricotta cheese, crumbled *
5–6 basil leaves, shredded

Method

1 Cook the pasta so it is ready when the sauce is cooked.
2 Heat the oil in a pan and gently cook the garlic and aubergine for 5 minutes. Add the tomatoes and seasoning and leave to cook over a low heat for 20 minutes, stirring from time to time.
3 Drain the spaghetti and put into a serving dish. Pour the sauce over the pasta then add the ricotta and basil. Mix well and serve.

---

* *The majority of ricotta cheese is soft and unripened, rather like a low-fat soft cheese. A firm variety is also available, with a fuller flavour and slightly crumbly texture.*

SPAGHETTI WITH CLAMS

MEDIUM-CALORIE DISH

Ingredients

1 lb (450 g) frozen shelled cooked clams or
4½ lb (2 kg) fresh clams
11 oz (320 g) spaghetti
2 tablespoons olive oil
1 clove garlic, finely chopped
2 tablespoons dry white wine
7 oz (200 g) tinned peeled tomatoes
1 teaspoon tomato purée
salt and black pepper to taste
1 sprig parsley, chopped

Method

1 If using frozen clams, remove from packet and leave to defrost in a dish.
2 Purge fresh clams by soaking overnight in a bucket of cold water with a little oatmeal added.
3 Scrub the clams, discarding any open ones or broken shells. Cook in a small amount of water in a covered saucepan for about 7–10 minutes until the shells open. Drain, keeping the water in reserve. Discard any unopened clams.
4 Put 10 clams to one side for decoration. Remove the clams from the shells of the remainder and put in a dish, rinsing off any sand that may be left. Chop the clams if very large.

5 Cook the pasta so it is ready when the sauce is cooked.

6 Heat the oil in a pan and cook the garlic for 2 minutes. Add the clams and white wine, then stir in the tomatoes and tomato purée. Add a few teaspoons of the reserved clam cooking liquid, or water, salt lightly and cook on a medium heat for 20 minutes. Stir from time to time and add a little extra liquid if necessary.

7 Drain the spaghetti and place in a serving dish. Add the sauce and sprinkle with the parsley and black pepper. Mix well and serve.

SPAGHETTI WITH CAPERS
AND BLACK OLIVES

MEDIUM-CALORIE DISH

Ingredients

11 oz (320 g) spaghetti
2 tablespoons olive oil
1 14-oz (400-g) tin peeled tomatoes, drained and
finely chopped
salt and black pepper to taste
3 teaspoons capers, chopped
15 pitted black olives, chopped
1 pinch crushed dried red chillies

Method

1 Cook the pasta so it is ready when the sauce is cooked.
2 Heat the oil in a saucepan and add the tomatoes. Season and simmer over a low heat for 10 minutes.
3 Add the capers, olives and chilli, and continue to cook for 10–15 minutes.
4 Drain the spaghetti, place in a serving dish and add the sauce. Mix well and serve.

SPAGHETTI WITH TOMATO AND BASIL SAUCE

MEDIUM-CALORIE DISH

Ingredients

½ 18-oz (500-g) carton passata or 1 lb (450 g) ripe
tomatoes
11 oz (320 g) spaghetti
1¼ oz (50 g) butter
salt and black pepper to taste
5–6 basil leaves, shredded
2 tablespoons grated Parmesan cheese

Method

1 If using fresh tomatoes, first peel them by plunging
briefly into boiling water. Blend in a liquidiser or food
processor then strain through a sieve over a bowl.
2 Cook the pasta so it is ready when the sauce is
cooked.
3 Melt the butter in a saucepan. Add the passata or
sieved tomatoes, season and simmer over a low heat
for 20 minutes. Cover the pan to prevent the sauce
from spitting out or evaporating.
4 Drain the spaghetti and place in a serving dish. Add
the sauce, basil and Parmesan. Mix well and serve.

BAKED MACARONI

MEDIUM-CALORIE DISH

Ingredients

11 oz (320 g) macaroni
1 oz (30 g) butter
1 oz (30 g) plain flour
1 vegetable stock cube, crumbled
1 pint (600 ml) semi-skimmed milk
grated nutmeg to taste
6 tablespoons grated Parmesan cheese
1 teaspoon olive oil

Method

1 Preheat the oven to 400°F (200°C, Gas Mark 6).
2 Cook the pasta so it is ready when the sauce is cooked.
3 Melt the butter in a small pan. Stir in the flour and stock cube. Slowly add the milk over a low heat, stirring constantly until the sauce thickens. Take off the heat and add a little grated nutmeg and two-thirds of the cheese.
4 Lightly oil an ovenproof dish, then pour in the well-drained pasta and cover with the sauce. Sprinkle over the remaining Parmesan cheese and put in the oven to brown for 20–30 minutes. Serve hot.

PASTA AND PULSES

MEDIUM-CALORIE DISH

Ingredients

5 oz (150 g) dried pulses, such as borlotti beans or
chick peas
3 tablespoons olive oil
1 clove garlic, finely chopped
1¼ oz (50 g) bacon, diced
2 tablespoons tinned chopped tomatoes
2 vegetable stock cubes, crumbled
3 tablespoons tomato purée
5 oz (150 g) small pasta shapes
1 sprig parsley, chopped
2 tablespoons grated Parmesan cheese

Method

1 Soak the pulses in cold water for about 12 hours.
Drain and rinse. Add to 3½ pints (2 litres) boiling
water, boil hard for 10 minutes and then simmer for
1–1½ hours, until tender. Drain and keep the water.
2 Put half the pulses through the food processor.
3 Heat 2 tablespoons oil in a pan and cook the garlic
and bacon. Add the tomatoes, stock cubes, whole
pulses and tomato purée. Stir and cook over a gentle
heat for 5 minutes, then add the pureéd pulses and
reserved cooking water and bring to the boil.
4 Add the pasta and cook for 15 minutes.
5 Serve with the parsley, cheese and remaining oil.

Rice Dishes

MUSHROOM RICE

HIGH-CALORIE DISH

Ingredients

7 oz (200 g) fresh wild mushrooms (such as caps or
porcini) or ¼ oz (20 g) dried wild mushrooms *

3 oz (90 g) butter

1 clove garlic, peeled

salt and black pepper to taste

11 oz (320 g) risotto rice

1 vegetable stock cube

3½ fl oz (100 ml) dry white wine

2 oz (60 g) Parmesan cheese, grated

2 sprigs parsley, chopped

* If wild mushrooms are not available, substitute brown-cap or
chestnut mushrooms.

Method

1 If using dried mushrooms, soak in a covering of cold/hot water for 30/15 minutes. Drain well, strain the liquid through muslin to remove any grit, then reserve it for use when cooking the rice. Finely slice the mushrooms.

2 If using fresh mushrooms, remove the stalks, wash quickly to prevent them becoming waterlogged, dry on kitchen paper and cut into slices.

3 Melt half the butter in a flameproof casserole. Add the whole clove of garlic and the mushrooms, and cook gently until the mushrooms are soft.

4 In a saucepan heat 1¼ pints (750 ml) lightly salted water.

5 Add the rice to the mushrooms, mixing well to ensure the grains are evenly coated.

6 Moisten the mixture with a ladleful of boiling water from the saucepan and continue to cook over a high heat.

7 Crumble in the stock cube, then add the wine, allowing it to evaporate over a high heat.

8 Gradually stir in the rest of the water, a ladleful at a time, and cook for about 40 minutes, or until all the liquid is absorbed.

9 Add the remaining butter, the cheese, parsley and black pepper.

10 Mix thoroughly, remove the garlic if desired and serve.

SHELLFISH RISOTTO

MEDIUM-CALORIE DISH

Ingredients

3½ oz (100 g) clams

3½ oz (100 g) mussels

2 cleaned squid and 2 cleaned octopuses *or* 4 cleaned
squid

2 tablespoons olive oil

1 clove garlic, finely chopped

7 oz (200 g) tomatoes, peeled and chopped

salt

11 oz (320 g) risotto rice

1 sprig parsley, chopped

Method

1 Discarding any open or broken shellfish, put the
well-washed clams and mussels into a saucepan of
boiling water. Allow the shells to open and discard any
whose shells do not.

2 Drain and rinse well.

3 Cut the squid and octopus into rings and small
pieces.

4 Heat the oil in a pan and gently cook the garlic. Add
the squid and octopus and the tomatoes.

5 Cook over a low heat for 10 minutes, then add the
mussels and clams and cook for a further 10 minutes.

6 In a saucepan heat 1¼ pints (750 ml) lightly salted
water.

7 Add the rice to the shellfish mixture and stir well. Increase the heat, then gradually add the boiling water a ladleful at a time, stirring constantly.

8 When the rice is soft, remove from heat, add the parsley and serve.

PARMESAN RISOTTO

MEDIUM-CALORIE DISH

Ingredients

1¼ pints (750 ml) good meat stock
3½ oz (100 g) butter
1 small onion, finely chopped
11 oz (320 g) risotto rice
1¾ oz (50 g) Parmesan cheese, grated

Method

1 Heat the stock, seasoning with salt if necessary.
2 Melt half the butter in a pan and gently cook the onion until golden.
3 Increase the heat, add the rice and mix well to coat all the grains.
4 Gradually add the hot stock, ladle by ladle, and continue to cook, stirring all the time, until the stock has been absorbed.
5 Turn off the heat. Add the remaining butter and the Parmesan cheese, mix well and serve hot.

Soups

VEGETABLE MINESTRONE
LOW-CALORIE DISH

Ingredients
2 tablespoons olive oil
1½ oz (40 g) bacon, diced
2 medium-sized potatoes, cut into cubes
10 oz (300 g) carrots, cut into cubes
1 medium-sized onion, sliced
2 sticks celery, sliced
1 leek, sliced
1 clove garlic, sliced
7 oz (200 g) drained, tinned borlotti beans
3½ oz (100 g) fresh peas or 3 oz (90 g) dried peas
5 oz (150 g) courgettes, cut into cubes
3½ oz (100 g) spinach leaves, shredded
2 large ripe plum tomatoes, thinly sliced
salt and black pepper to taste
5–6 basil leaves, shredded
2 tablespoons grated Parmesan cheese

Method
1 Heat the oil in a very large pan and cook the bacon. Add the potatoes, carrots, onion, celery, leek and garlic, cover and cook over a low heat for 15 minutes, stirring from time to time.
2 Stir in the beans, peas, courgettes, spinach and tomatoes, and cook for a further 10 minutes.

3 Pour in 3½ pints (2 litres) water, season with salt and bring to the boil. Lower the heat and simmer for 1–1½ hours, adding the basil a few minutes before the end.
4 Serve with grated cheese and pepper to taste.

ONION SOUP

LOW-CALORIE DISH

Ingredients

2 vegetable stock cubes
1 oz (30 g) butter
5 medium-sized onions, finely chopped
1 tablespoon plain flour
4 slices bread
1¾ oz (50 g) Emmenthal cheese, thinly sliced
1 tablespoon grated Parmesan cheese
black pepper to taste

Method

1 Heat 1¾ pints (1 litre) water in a saucepan and add the stock cubes.
2 In a large pan, melt the butter and cook the onions over a low heat for 10 minutes, stirring constantly.
3 Sprinkle over the flour, mix well, add the stock and simmer over a low heat for 20–30 minutes.
4 Preheat the oven to 350°F (180°C, Gas Mark 4).
5 Toast the bread, place one slice in each ovenproof bowl, and top with the Emmenthal cheese.
6 Spoon the onion soup carefully into the bowls. Sprinkle with the Parmesan and a generous amount of black pepper.
7 Bake in the oven for about 20 minutes.

VEGETABLE BROTH

MEDIUM-CALORIE DISH

Ingredients

2 medium-sized potatoes
1 small carrot
1 plum tomato
1 small onion
1 stick celery
1¼ oz (50 g) spinach leaves
3 leaves savoy cabbage
1¼ oz (50 g) tinned borlotti beans
2½ oz (70 g) fresh peas
1 clove garlic, finely chopped
1 sprig parsley
1 teaspoon tomato purée
2 vegetable stock cubes

Method

1 Cut the vegetables into large pieces and coarsely shred the leaves.
2 Heat 2 pints (1.15 litres) water. Add all the vegetables, the garlic, parsley, tomato purée and crumbled stock cubes, and simmer for 30 minutes.
3 Remove the vegetables with a slotted metal spoon. Put them through a liquidiser or a food processor, and pour the resulting mixture back into the broth. Taste, adding salt if necessary, and bring back to the boil.
4 Serve with the croûtons and grated cheese.

STACCIATELLA
LOW-CALORIE DISH

Ingredients
28 fl oz (800 ml) good chicken stock
1½ oz (40 g) butter
4 slices Ciabatta, Pugliese or other Italian bread
4 eggs
4 tablespoons grated Parmesan cheese
salt
grated nutmeg to taste

Method
1 Heat the stock in a saucepan.
2 Melt the butter in a large pan. When it starts to froth, add the slices of bread and allow to become golden.
3 Beat the eggs in a bowl, then add the cheese, salt and nutmeg, and mix well.
4 When the stock is at boiling point, whisk in the egg mixture. Leave to cook for a couple of minutes until the egg has set in flakes.
5 Place the bread in serving dishes and pour over the soup.

Fish Dishes

Fish is an important part of a healthy diet, especially white fish, which has a low fat content. Please note that some of the following recipes can be adapted to use available fish. For example, thicker fillets of cod or haddock may be used instead of swordfish, and mackerel can often be used in place of sardines.

WHITING IN TARTARE SAUCE
MEDIUM-CALORIE DISH

Ingredients
1½ lb (700 g) whiting fillets
salt
1 small onion
1 medium-sized carrot, halved
1 stick celery, cut into chunks
1 bay leaf
2 eggs
5 tablespoons olive oil
2 teaspoons capers, finely chopped
4 small gherkins, finely chopped
2 sprigs parsley, finely chopped
2 teaspoons white wine vinegar

Method

1 Bring to the boil 1¾ pints (1 litre) salted water.

2 Remove the outer layer of onion flesh and set aside. Add the remaining whole onion to the water with the carrot, celery and bay leaf. Boil over a medium heat for 10 minutes.

3 Add the fish and cook over a medium heat for 10–12 minutes.

4 Remove and drain the fish, discarding the skin and any bones, and divide into portions. Place on four individual plates.

5 Hard-boil the eggs, shell and place the yolks in a bowl. Mash with a wooden spoon and mix in the oil, a teaspoon at a time, until you have a smooth, creamy sauce.

6 Very finely chop the reserved onion. Add to the sauce with the capers, gherkin, parsley, finely chopped egg whites, wine vinegar and salt to taste. Mix well and spoon over the fish. Leave to marinate for about 3 hours before serving.

FISH FILLETS IN REMOULADE SAUCE

LOW-CALORIE DISH

Ingredients

1 small onion, quartered

1 medium-sized carrot, quartered

1 stick celery, quartered

2 bay leaves

1 lb (450 g) mixed white fish fillets

(whiting, cod or monkfish, for example)

1 egg yolk

juice of 1 lemon

salt

¼ pint (150 ml) olive oil

4 small gherkins

1 teaspoon capers

3 sprigs parsley

Method

1 Bring 1 pint (600 ml) water to the boil in the base of a steamer. Add the onion (reserving an inner 'leaf'), the carrot, celery and bay leaf. Cover and boil for 5 minutes.

2 Steam the fish over the boiling vegetables for 8–12 minutes, depending on the thickness of the fillets. Place on a serving dish and leave to cool.

3 Place the egg yolk in a bowl, add the lemon juice, season to taste and mix. Beat in the oil a few drops at a time, to make a mayonnaise.

4 Finely chop the onion 'leaf', the gherkins, capers and parsley, and place in a clean napkin, squeezing hard to eliminate all the liquid. Add to the mayonnaise and mix well.

5 Spoon the sauce over the fish and leave to stand for 30 minutes before serving.

FILLETS OF SOLE IN BREADCRUMBS

LOW-CALORIE DISH

Ingredients

2 sprigs parsley, chopped
1 clove garlic, finely chopped
4 tablespoons fresh white breadcrumbs
salt and black pepper to taste
2 tablespoons olive oil
1 lb (450 g) lemon sole fillets
1 lemon

Method

1 Preheat the oven to 400°F (200°C, Gas Mark 6).

2 Mix together the parsley, garlic and breadcrumbs, and season to taste.

3 Grease an ovenproof dish with a little of the oil and place the fillets in it. Sprinkle with the parsley and breadcrumb mixture and trickle over the rest of the oil.

4 Bake in the oven for 20–25 minutes and serve with a slice of lemon.

BRAISED WHITING

LOW-CALORIE DISH

Ingredients

4 slices rindless bacon
4 small whiting, gutted and heads removed
2 tablespoons olive oil
1 medium-sized onion, chopped
1 stick celery, chopped
1 small carrot, chopped
1 sprig rosemary, chopped
1 clove garlic, finely chopped
1 tablespoon tinned chopped tomatoes
3½ fl oz (100 ml) light red wine
1 teaspoon flour
salt and black pepper to taste

Method

1 Wrap a slice of bacon around each fish and fix in place with a wooden cocktail stick.

2 Heat the oil in a large, deep frying pan or flameproof casserole and gently cook the vegetables, rosemary and garlic for 10 minutes.

3 Place the fish in the pan and cook briefly on both sides. Add the tomatoes.

4 Mix together the wine and flour, pour over the fish and season to taste.

5 Cover and simmer over a low heat for 20 minutes, turning the fish a couple of times. Serve immediately.

SWORDFISH WITH OLIVES

LOW-CALORIE DISH

Ingredients

3 tablespoons olive oil

1 clove garlic, finely chopped

1 small onion, finely chopped

14 oz (400 g) swordfish steak, cut into 4 pieces

1 teaspoon capers

5–6 pitted black olives, halved

coarsely grated rind of ½ lemon

salt and black pepper

7 fl oz (200 ml) dry white wine

1 sprig parsley, finely chopped

Method

1 Heat the oil in a large, deep frying pan or flameproof casserole and gently cook the garlic and onion. Add the swordfish and cook until golden brown on both sides.

2 Add the capers, olives, lemon rind, seasoning and white wine, and cook over a medium heat for 15 minutes, turning the fish a couple of times.

3 Remove the fish and place on a serving dish. Sprinkle with the parsley and a pinch of black pepper. Cover and keep warm.

4 Boil the sauce, stirring until reduced by half, then pour over the fish and serve.

BAKED TROUT

LOW-CALORIE DISH

Ingredients

4 trout, cleaned
2–3 sage leaves, shredded
1 sprig rosemary, chopped
1 clove garlic, finely chopped
salt and black pepper to taste
1 lemon, thinly sliced
3½ fl oz (100 ml) olive oil
1 tablespoon white wine vinegar
1 teaspoon capers, chopped

Method

1 Preheat the oven to 400°F (200°C, Gas Mark 6).
2 Place each trout on a large piece of aluminium foil or greaseproof paper. Sprinkle with the herbs and garlic, season to taste and lay over slices of lemon. Wrap the fish parcels securely, place in an ovenproof dish and bake for 30–40 minutes.
3 To make the dressing put the oil and vinegar into a dish, add the capers, season to taste and beat with a fork.
4 Serve the dressing separately with the fish.

MESSINA-STYLE SARDINES

MEDIUM-CALORIE DISH

Ingredients

3½ oz (100 g) fresh white breadcrumbs
2 oz (60 g) soft sheep's milk or goat's cheese
1 clove garlic, finely chopped
3–4 mint leaves, finely chopped
2 tablespoons olive oil
salt and black pepper to taste
8 large fresh sardines, filleted
juice of 1 lemon

Method

1 Preheat the oven to 400°C (200°C, Gas Mark 6).
2 To make the stuffing, mix the breadcrumbs with the cheese, garlic, mint and oil, seasoning to taste.
3 Grease an ovenproof dish and place in half the sardine fillets, skin side down.
4 Spoon the stuffing over the sardines, cover with the remaining fillets, skin side up, and press down gently. Season to taste and bake for about 20–30 minutes.
5 Halfway through cooking, squeeze the lemon juice over the fish.
6 Serve hot.

BAKED TUNA
MEDIUM-CALORIE DISH

Ingredients
4 portions tuna steak, skinned
salt and black pepper to taste
2 tablespoons olive oil
4 slices lemon
16 pitted black olives
4 drained, canned anchovy fillets rolled
to enclose a caper

Method
1 Preheat the oven to 425°F (220°C, Gas Mark 7).
2 Place each tuna portion on a large piece of aluminium foil or greaseproof paper.
3 Sprinkle with salt and pepper and pour on a little oil. Place a slice of lemon, 4 olives and an anchovy roll on top of each one.
4 Wrap the cutlets securely, place in an ovenproof dish and bake for 25–35 minutes.
5 Serve in the foil.

LIVORNO TROUT

LOW-CALORIE DISH

Ingredients

4 trout, cleaned

1 14-oz (400-g) tin peeled tomatoes

1 onion, chopped

14 fl oz (400 ml) dry white wine

salt and black pepper to taste

1 tablespoon finely chopped herbs (oregano or
marjoram give a distinctive flavour; parsley
is more delicate)

Method

1 Place the trout in a large, shallow pan with the tomatoes, onion, wine, seasoning and herbs.

2 Cook over a medium heat, turning after 10 minutes. Remove the fish when cooked, about 20 minutes, depending on size.

3 Reduce the sauce by boiling hard, pour over the fish and serve hot or warm.

SICILIAN-STYLE SWORDFISH

MEDIUM-CALORIE DISH

Ingredients

2 tablespoons olive oil
2 cloves garlic, crushed
4 portions swordfish steak
1 1¾-oz (50-g) can anchovy fillets, drained and finely
chopped.
½ 18-oz (500-g) carton passata or 1 lb (450 g)
tomatoes, peeled and liquidised
8 pitted black olives
1 teaspoon capers
salt and black pepper to taste

Method

1 Heat the oil in a large pan, add the garlic and
swordfish and cook gently for 5–10 minutes, turning
the fish once.
2 When both sides of the fish are golden, add the
anchovies, passata or tomatoes, olives and capers.
Cover and cook gently for 15 minutes.
3 Season and serve.

SOLE IN MIMOSA

LOW-CALORIE DISH

Ingredients

1½ oz (40 g) butter
4 lemon sole fillets
1 tablespoon flour
½ pint (300 ml) dry white wine
salt and pepper to taste
1 oz (30 g) Parmesan cheese, grated
grated rind of ½ lemon

Method

1 Melt the butter in a flameproof serving dish.
2 Dust the fillets with the flour, add to the pan and cook gently on both sides until just firm.
3 Pour in the wine, season to taste and poach gently for a further 10 minutes, basting with the wine.
4 Sprinkle with the cheese and lemon rind.
5 Leave to stand for a couple of minutes and then serve.

PEPPERS WITH TUNA PATE

MEDIUM-CALORIE DISH

Ingredients

1 7-oz (200-g) tin tuna in brine
4 oz (120 g) softened butter
1 teaspoon capers
4 drained, tinned anchovy
juice of ½ lemon
1 red and 1 yellow pepper

Method

1 To make the pâté, put the drained tuna, butter, capers, anchovies and lemon juice in a liquidiser or food processor for 2–3 minutes, until the mixture becomes smooth and creamy.

2 Blanch the peppers in boiling water for 5 minutes then halve lengthways and remove the seeds and core. Cool.

3 Spoon the pâté into the pepper halves.

4 Refrigerate for 2–3 hours before serving.

Meat Dishes

ROMAN-STYLE VEAL ESCALOPES
LOW-CALORIE DISH

Ingredients
4 3½-oz (100-g) veal escalopes
4 3-oz (90-g) slices prosucitto ham
4 large sage leaves
1½ oz (40 g) butter
2 tablespoons dry white wine
salt and black pepper to taste

Method
1 Flatten the veal escalopes with a rolling pin.
2 Put a slice of prosucitto and a sage leaf on each escalope and fix in place with a wooden toothpick.
3 Melt the butter in a large pan and add the meat, cooking for 5 minutes on each side.
4 Add the wine and season to taste. After 2 minutes turn the meat again and allow to cook for a further 2 minutes. Serve at once.

CHICKEN BREAST IN GREEN SAUCE

LOW-CALORIE DISH

Ingredients

1 teaspoon capers, chopped

3 small gherkins, chopped

4 pitted green olives, chopped

1 sprig parsley, chopped

3–4 basil leaves, shredded

3 tablespoons olive oil

4 chicken breast fillets

1–2 tablespoons flour

½ oz (15 g) butter

2 tablespoons dry white wine

Method

1 To make the green sauce, pound together the capers, gherkins, olives, parsley and basil and mix with 2 tablespoons oil. Season with black pepper.

2 Coat the chicken breasts in flour.

3 In a pan, heat the remaining oil with the butter. Cook the chicken breast fillets on both sides until golden brown.

4 Add the wine and a little salt and cook over a low heat for 10–12 minutes, turning occasionally, until the chicken is cooked through.

5 Place on a serving dish. When warm, spread over the green sauce and leave to marinate for at least an hour, turning a couple of times.

6 Serve with vegetables or a salad.

CHICKEN IN LEMON

LOW-CALORIE DISH

Ingredients

4 chicken portions
salt and black pepper to taste
2 lemons
1 teaspoon olive oil

Method

1 Preheat the oven to 400°F (200°C, Gas Mark 6).
2 Place the chicken portions in a deep dish and sprinkle lightly with salt. Add the juice of one of the lemons. Leave to marinate for 15 minutes, turning a couple of times.
3 Cut the second lemon into 8 slices.
4 Grease an ovenproof dish with the oil. Place 4 slices of lemon in the dish, and a piece of chicken on top of each one. Then lay a second lemon slice on top of each chicken portion, and bake for 45 minutes, or until the chicken is cooked through.
5 Halfway through cooking, sprinkle the juice from the marinade over the chicken.
6 Serve seasoned with black pepper.

ROAST TURKEY IN WHITE WINE

LOW-CALORIE DISH

Ingredients
1 tablespoon flour
14 oz (400 g) turkey slices
2 tablespoons olive oil
4–5 sage leaves
3½ fl oz (100 ml) white wine
1 vegetable stock cube

Method
1 Flour the turkey slices.
2 Heat the oil in a large pan. Add the sage leaves and cook the turkey slices over a high heat until both sides are golden brown.
3 Reduce the heat, add the wine and a crumbled stock cube, and cook for 20 minutes, turning once. If necessary, turn up the heat to reduce the sauce.
4 Serve hot.

TURKEY ALLA FIORENTINA

LOW-CALORIE DISH

Ingredients

1 teaspoon capers
2 tablespoons olive oil
14 oz (400 g) turkey slices
1 clove garlic, finely chopped
10 pitted black olives, finely chopped
1 sprig parsley, finely chopped
1 14-oz (400-g) tin chopped tomatoes
salt to taste

Method

1 Rinse the capers, dry and finely chop.
2 Heat the oil in a large pan and lightly brown the turkey slices on both sides over a high heat.
3 Lower the heat. Sprinkle over the garlic, capers, olives and parsley, add the tomatoes and salt and mix well.
4 Cover the pan and cook gently for 15 minutes, turning the turkey slices a couple of times. Serve hot.

POLENTA WITH MEAT SAUCE

HIGH-CALORIE DISH

Polenta is like a sort of thick porridge made with maize flour. This recipe comes from the north of Italy and is one of Beppe Signori's favourites.

Ingredients

salt
10 oz (300 g) maize flour
1 tablespoon olive oil
¼ oz (7 g) butter
1 small onion, chopped
1½ oz (40 g) bacon, diced
2 oz (60 g) fresh Italian sausage
(see footnote, page 83)
3½ oz (100 g) minced beef
2 teaspoons dry white wine
7 oz (200 g) tinned peeled tomatoes
1 teaspoon tomato purée
black pepper
3 tablespoons grated Parmesan cheese

Method

1 In a high-sided pan, bring to the boil 2 pints (1.5 litres) salted water.

2 To make the polenta, add the maize flour to the boiling water in a thin stream, mixing well to prevent lumps. Continue to cook for about 40 minutes, stirring constantly until the mixture comes away from the sides of the pan. Turn into a shallow dish to cool and set.

3 Heat the oil and butter in a separate pan and gently cook the onion, then the bacon, sausage and minced beef.

4 After 10 minutes, add the wine and allow to evaporate over a high heat. Add the tomatoes, tomato purée and season to taste. Cover and cook over a low heat for 20–30 minutes, stirring occasionally.

5 Cut the polenta into pieces and serve on a round, wooden dish. Place a portion in each individual serving dish and top with the meat sauce and grated cheese.

Egg dishes

SWALLOW'S NEST EGGS
MEDIUM-CALORIE DISH

Ingredients
2 lb (1 kg) spinach
2 oz (60 g) butter
2 tablespoons grated Parmesan cheese
salt and black pepper to taste
grated nutmeg
4 eggs

Method
1 Preheat the oven to 350°F (180°C, Gas Mark 4).
2 Cook and drain the spinach. Put into a pan with three-quarters of the butter and most of the Parmesan cheese. Add a pinch of salt and a little grated nutmeg, and mix well.
3 Spoon the mixture into a greased, shallow ovenproof dish, spreading it out to cover the base. Make four holes in the mixture. Place a knob of butter then break an egg into each one.
4 Bake for about 10 minutes, until the eggs are cooked.
5 Season with salt, pepper and a little Parmesan cheese. Serve hot.

EGGS WITH MOZZARELLA

LOW-CALORIE DISH

Ingredients

1 oz (30 g) butter
4 eggs
1 oz (30 g) mozzarella cheese, sliced
salt and black pepper to taste

Method

1 Melt the butter in a large pan and fry the eggs.
2 When almost cooked, cover each egg with one or two slices of mozzarella. Put the lid on the pan and turn off the heat. The cheese will melt on top of the eggs.
3 Season with salt and pepper and serve.

Vegetable dishes

CARROTS WITH PARMESAN CHEESE
LOW-CALORIE DISH

Ingredients
salt
1 lb (450 g) carrots
1 oz (30 g) butter
2 tablespoons grated Parmesan cheese

Method
1 Bring to the boil 3½ pints (2 litres) salted water.
2 Top and tail the carrots, scrape or scrub clean and add to the boiling water. Cook for 10 minutes, then drain and cut into round slices.
3 Melt the butter in a large pan, add the sliced carrots and cook for 10 minutes over a gentle heat.
4 Sprinkle the cheese over the carrots and continue to cook for 5 minutes. Serve at once.

CAULIFLOWER CHEESE

LOW-CALORIE DISH

Ingredients

1 medium cauliflower
1 oz (30 g) butter
1 oz (30 g) flour
14 fl oz (400 ml) semi-skimmed milk
salt to taste
5 tablespoons grated Parmesan or Pecorino cheese

Method

1 Preheat the oven to 400°F (200°C, Gas Mark 6).
2 Break the cauliflower into large florets, and steam or boil in minimum water for about 15 minutes.
3 Melt the butter in a saucepan. Add the flour and cook for a couple of minutes. Gradually pour in the milk, season with salt and thicken the sauce over a low heat, stirring constantly. Remove from the heat and stir in most of the cheese.
4 Drain the cauliflower. Place in an ovenproof dish and pour over the sauce. Sprinkle with the remaining cheese.
5 Bake for 20 minutes, or until the top is golden brown.

GREEN BEANS WITH TOMATOES

LOW-CALORIE DISH

Ingredients

salt
1 lb (450 g) green beans
½ oz (15 g) butter
1 small onion, chopped
1 14-oz (400-g) tin peeled tomatoes, drained and
finely chopped
3–4 sage leaves, shredded

Method

1 Bring to the boil 3½ pints (2 litres) salted water.
2 Top, tail and string the beans. Drop into the boiling water and cook for about 10 minutes.
3 Melt the butter in a pan and gently cook the onion until softened.
4 Add the tomatoes and sage and heat through.
5 Drain the beans and add to the sauce.
6 Cook over a gentle heat for 10–15 minutes, stirring occasionally. Serve hot or cold.

BAKED FENNEL

LOW-CALORIE DISH

Ingredients
salt
2 medium-sized bulbs fennel
1 teaspoon olive oil
2 tablespoons grated Parmesan cheese
½ oz (15 g) butter

Method
1 Preheat the oven to 400°F (200°C, Gas Mark 6).
2 Clean the fennel, removing the outside leaves and green stalks. Cut into ½-inch (1-cm) slices and cook in minimum boiling water until just firm.
3 Drain the fennel and layer in an ovenproof dish rubbed with oil. Sprinkle with the cheese and dot with knobs of butter.
4 Cook for 20–25 minutes, or until the top is golden brown.

AUBERGINES AND TOMATOES

LOW-CALORIE DISH

Ingredients

2 medium-sized aubergines
5 tablespoons olive oil
1 clove garlic, peeled
1 sprig rosemary
1 tablespoons tinned chopped tomatoes
salt and black pepper to taste
2–3 sprigs parsley, chopped

Method

1 Cut the aubergines into small.

2 Heat the oil in a large pan and gently cook the garlic and rosemary.

3 Add the aubergine cubes and mix well with a wooden spoon. Stir in the tomatoes, then season, cover and leave to cook over a gentle heat for 20 minutes, stirring occasionally.

4 Add the parsley just before turning off the heat.

5 Remove the garlic and rosemary before serving.

CHEESY BAKED VEGETABLES

LOW-CALORIE DISH

Ingredients

1½ lb (675 g) potatoes
10 oz (300 g) carrots
salt and black pepper to taste
1½ oz (40 g) butter
1½ oz (40 g) flour
1 pint (600 ml) semi-skimmed milk
2 tablespoons grated Parmesan cheese

Method

1 Preheat the oven to 400°F (200°C, Gas Mark 6).
2 Cook the potatoes and carrots separately in salted water until just firm. Do not peel or chop.
3 To make the sauce, melt the butter in a pan and stir in the flour. Add the milk and cook over a low heat, stirring to make a sauce. Season to taste.
4 Drain the vegetables. Peel and slice the potatoes, and slice the carrots (peeling only if necessary).
5 Place about a quarter of the sauce in a deep ovenproof dish, then add a layer of potatoes followed by a layer of carrots to create diverse colours. Continue to create layers in this way until all the vegetables and sauce are used up.
6 Finish the layers with sauce and sprinkle with the cheese.
7 Bake for 20 minutes until the top is golden brown.

CREAMED SPINACH

LOW-CALORIE DISH

Ingredients

1 lb (450 g) frozen chopped spinach
1¼ oz (50 g) butter
1 oz (30 g) flour
14 fl oz (400 ml) semi-skimmed milk
salt and black pepper to taste

Method

1 Preheat the oven to 400°F (200°C, Gas Mark 6).

2 Place the frozen spinach in a saucepan with ¾ oz (20 g) butter, cover and cook over a low heat for 15 minutes, stirring occasionally.

3 In another saucepan melt the remaining butter. Stirring constantly over a low heat, add the flour then the milk. Cook until the sauce thickens and season with salt.

4 Uncover the spinach and, if necessary, turn up the heat to allow some of the liquid to evaporate.

5 Combine the spinach and sauce and place in an ovenproof dish, sprinkling black pepper on top.

6 Cook through for 10 minutes in the oven and serve hot.

COURGETTES AND TOMATOES

LOW-CALORIE DISH

Ingredients

3 tablespoons olive oil
1 small clove garlic, crushed
1 lb (450 g) courgettes, sliced
1 tablespoon tinned chopped tomatoes
salt and black pepper to taste
1 sprig parsley, chopped

Method

1 Heat the oil in a straight-sided pan. Cook the garlic and courgettes for 5 minutes
2 Stir in the tomatoes, season, cover and cook for 20 minutes over a low heat, stirring occasionally. Add a little water if necessary.
3 Sprinkle with parsley and serve.

POLISH ASPARAGUS

MEDIUM-CALORIE DISH

Ingredients
2 lb (1 kg) asparagus
salt
4 eggs, hard-boiled
2 sprigs parsley, chopped
3½ oz (100 g) butter

Method

1 Trim the ends of the asparagus and lightly scrape the lower parts of the stems. Rinse under running water.

2 Cook the stems upright in a saucepan of salted water for 20–25 minutes, until the tips are soft to the touch. Make sure the water comes no higher than the white part of the asparagus.

3 Shell the eggs. Separate the whites from the yolks, then mash the yolks with a fork. Finely chop the whites. Add the parsley to the egg yolks.

4 Drain the asparagus, put onto individual plates and sprinkle with the egg mixture.

5 Melt the butter, season lightly with salt and pour over the asparagus. Serve immediately.

Desserts

AMARETTI CREAM
MEDIUM-CALORIE DISH

Ingredients
¾ pint (450 ml) full-cream milk
pared rind of 1 lemon
4 egg yolks
2 oz (60 g) caster sugar
1½ oz (40 g) plain flour
6–7 amaretti biscuits, crushed
1 teaspoon vanilla essence

Method
1 Gently heat the milk in a saucepan, flavouring with the lemon rind. Do not allow to boil.
2 Whisk the egg yolks with the sugar in a large bowl until thickened and pale yellow in colour.
3 Add the sifted flour, biscuits and vanilla and fold in. Stir in the milk gradually and then return to the pan.
4 Remove the lemon rind, and allow the mixture to thicken over a low heat, stirring constantly.
5 Pour the cream into a serving dish or individual dishes and chill before serving.

APPLES WITH ALMONDS

MEDIUM-CALORIE DISH

Ingredients

2½ oz (70 g) blanched almonds
4 dessert apples
lemon juice
¼ oz (7 g) butter
2 tablespoons caster sugar
¼ pint (150 ml) sweet dessert wine
3 oz (90 g) apricot jam

Method

1 Preheat the oven to 350°F (180°C, Gas Mark 4).

2 Roast the almonds in the oven for 2–3 minutes, then cool and chop into small pieces.

3 Peel, core and thickly slice the apples. Sprinkle with a little lemon juice to prevent discoloration.

4 Grease an ovenproof dish with butter and sprinkle with half the sugar. Place the apple slices in the dish, slightly overlapping.

5 Pour the wine evenly over the apples, cover with foil and bake for 30 minutes.

6 Melt the jam gently in a saucepan, spread over the apples and return to the oven for a further 20 minutes, still covered.

7 Sprinkle with the almonds and remaining sugar and cook uncovered for 10 minutes.

8 Allow to cool a little before serving.

CHOCOLATE PEARS

MEDIUM-CALORIE DISH

Ingredients

2 large William pears
2 tablespoons dry white wine
1 tablespoon caster sugar
1 cinnamon stick, crumbled
1¾ oz (50 g) plain chocolate
2 teaspoons milk

Method

1 Peel and halve the pears. Place in a pan large enough to take the four halves without overlap. Add 3½ fl oz (100 ml) water and the wine.

2 Sprinkle with the sugar and pieces of cinnamon. Cover and cook gently for 15 minutes.

3 Melt the chocolate with the milk in a small bowl placed over a pan of boiling water.

4 Remove the pears from the cooking liquid, dry with kitchen paper and arrange on a serving dish.

5 Over a high heat reduce the cooking liquid by a third, sieve to remove the cinnamon pieces, then carefully stir into the melted chocolate, off the heat.

6 Pour the sauce over the pears and serve hot or warm as preferred.

SWEET KEBABS

LOW-CALORIE DISH

Ingredients

8 oz (230 g) strawberries, hulled
3 tablespoons icing sugar
1 teaspoon cider or raspberry vinegar
2 dessert apples
8 cocktail cherries

Method

1 Put the strawberries in a dish with the sugar and vinegar. Mix well and leave to stand for 10 minutes (this helps the strawberries maintain their flavour).
2 Peel the apples and cut into cubes.
3 Make kebabs by placing alternately on each skewer strawberries and cubes of apple, with a cherry at either end.
4 Serve at once.

STRAWBERRY FROTH

MEDIUM-CALORIE DISH

Ingredients
14 oz (400 g) strawberries
2 tablespoons icing sugar
1 tablespoon orange liqueur
(Cointreau, Grand Marnier)
½ pint (150 ml) whipping cream
2 egg whites

Method

1 Purée all but 6 or 7 of the strawberries in a liquidiser or food processor with the sugar and orange liqueur. Take care not to overliquidise them.

2 Place the pureé in a large bowl. Whip the cream and mix in.

3 Whisk the egg whites until stiff and fold in.

4 Place in a serving dish or individual dishes and chill before serving.

5. Decorate with the reserved strawberries before serving.

INDEX